ARCHAEOLOGICAL SURVEY OF INDIA

LISTS OF ANTIQUARIAN REMAINS IN THE CENTRAL PROVINCES AND BERAR

ARCHAEOLOGICAL SURVEY OF INDIA

LISTS OF ANTIQUARIAN REMAINS IN THE CENTRAL PROVINCES AND BERAR

COMPILED

BY

HENRY COUSENS, M.R.A.S.,

SUPERINTENDENT, ARCHAEOLOGICAL SURVEY, BOMBAY.

GYAN

Published by

Gyan Publishing House
5, Ansari Road
Daryaganj, New Delhi-110002
Phone: 011-47034999, 9811692060
E-mail: books@gyanbooks.com

Distribution Network
gyanbooks.com
India, USA, Canada, UK, Australia, France

ISBN : 978-81-212-2478-9 (HB)
First Published, 1897

2nd Impression 2021

Printed at: Gyan Press, Delhi.

Lists of
Antiquarian Remains in the Central Provinces and Berar Compiled
Author: Henry Cousens

ARCHÆOLOGICAL SURVEY OF INDIA.

LISTS OF

ANTIQUARIAN REMAINS

IN THE

CENTRAL PROVINCES AND BERÂR

COMPILED

BY

HENRY COUSENS, M.R.A.S.,

SUPERINTENDENT, ARCHÆOLOGICAL SURVEY, BOMBAY.

CALCUTTA:

OFFICE OF THE SUPERINTENDENT OF GOVERNMENT PRINTING, INDIA.

1897.

List of Volumes constituting the new Imperial series of the Reports of the Archæological Survey of India.

Prescribed number in new series.	Name of book.	Author or Editor.	Date (passed or proposed) of publication.	Provincial Number. Western India.	Southern India.	Northern India.
I	Report of the first season's operations in the Belgaum and Kaladgi Districts.	Burgess	1874	I	...	...
II	Report on the antiquities of Kathiawar and Kach	Burgess	1876	II	...	...
III	Report on the antiquities of the Bidar and Aurangabad Districts	Burgess	1878	III	...	...
IV	The Buddhist caves and their inscriptions	Burgess	1883	IV	...	...
V	The caves of Elura and the other Brahmanical and Jaina caves in Western India	Burgess	...	V	...	...
VI	The Buddhist Stupas of Amaravati and Jaggayyapeta	Burgess	1887	...	I	...
VII	Lists of Antiquarian Remains in the Presidency of Madras (Volume I)	Sewell	1882	...	II	...
VIII	Lists of Inscriptions and sketch of Dynasties of Southern India (Volume II)	Sewell	1884	...	III	...
IX	South Indian inscriptions (Volume I)	Hultzsch	1890	...	IV	...
X	Ditto ditto (Volume II)	Hultzsch	1891	...	V	...
XI	Report on the Sharqi Architecture of Jaunpur	Führer and Smith	1889	...	...	I
XII	Monumental antiquities and Inscriptions in the North-Western Provinces and Oudh	Führer	1891	...	...	II
XIII	Epigraphia Indica of the Archæological Survey of India (Volume I)	Burgess	1891	...	...	...
XIV	Epigraphia Indica of the Archæological Survey of India (Volume II)	Burgess	1893	...	...	...
XV	South Indian Buddhist antiquities	Rea	1894	...	VI	...
XVI	Revised List of antiquities, Bombay	Cousens	...	...	...	...
XVII	List of Architectural and Archæological Remains in Coorg	Rea	1894	...	VII	...
XVIII	Report on the Moghal Architecture of Fatehpur Sikri	Smith	1895	...	...	III
XIX	List of Monumental Antiquities and Inscriptions in the Central Provinces and Berar	Cousens	1897	...	...	IV
XX	Monograph on the Great Jaina establishment under the Kankali Tila Mathura	Führer	1896	...	...	V
XXI	Chalukyan Architecture including examples from the Ballari District in Madras	Rea	1896	...	VIII	...
XXII	Bower manuscripts	Hœrnle	1894	...	...	...
XXIII	Muhammadan Architecture in Gujrat	Burgess	1896	VI	...	...
XXIV	The Muhammadan Architecture of Ahmedabad	Burgess	1897	VII	...	...
XXV	Monumental Remains of the Dutch East India Company in the Presidency of Madras	Rea	1897	...	IX	...

PREFACE.

THESE Lists of Antiquarian Remains in the Central Provinces and Berâr are compiled from old manuscript and printed lists, very imperfect, General Sir Alexander Cunningham's Reports, the Central Provinces and Berâr Gazetteers, a short list in Dr. Burgess' Lists of Remains in the Bombay Presidency, additions and corrections received from District Officers, and information gleaned personally during two tours which I made in 1892-93-94 through portions of these districts. The orders of Government with regard to this compilation are contained in the Government of Bombay Resolutions in the General Department, Nos. 2355 of the 12th July, 3851 of the 24th October, 3912 of the 28th October, 1892, and in the Government of India letters in the Revenue and Agricultural Department (Archæology), Nos. $\frac{3553}{32}$ of the 8th August and $\frac{1447}{32}$ of the 19th October 1894.

This does not profess to be a perfect and exhaustive list and must be accepted as provisional, for there are still very large tracts in the Central Provinces which have not yet been examined by the antiquarian, and hardly by any one else. Owing, too, to the want of an elementary acquaintance with antiquarian remains, or even a passing interest in them, on the part of many District Officers, much of the information obtained from them is very defective, and many entries of uninteresting and modern objects have been included in their returns which should not have found a place at all. To avoid the possibility of removing genuine entries in weeding these out, in the absence of fuller information, I have allowed many doubtful ones to stand as they are.

The classification for conservation purposes, also, as indicated by the Roman numerals down the margins opposite each entry, is, in many instances, provisional, and it is hoped that District Officers and others will from time to time enter upon their copies of this volume all such corrections and additions as may be found necessary in view of the possible revision of the lists in the future.

Some names may be found incorrectly spelt. All sorts of spelling have been used in the various old lists and Gazetteers from which they have been taken. Before compilation rough lists were circulated among District Officers for additions or corrections. Since the final lists have been printed it was found necessary to refer again to those officers for the correct location of certain places for the maps, and this has in some instances brought forth new spelling and correction of names which were overlooked in the first instance, but have come too late to be used in the text.

For Conservation purposes all monuments have been classified as follows:—

I*a*.—*Monuments which, from their present condition and historical or archæological value, ought to be maintained in permanent good repair, and which are in possession or charge of Government, or in respect of which Government must undertake the cost of all measures of conservation.*

I*b*.—*Monuments of the same class, which are in possession or charge of private bodies or individuals.*

II*a*.—*Monuments which it is now only possible or desirable to save from further decay by such minor measures as the eradication of vegetation, the exclusion of water from the walls, and the like, such being in possession or charge of Government, or in respect of which Government must undertake the cost of such measures.*

II*b*.—*Monuments of the same class in possession of private bodies or individuals.*

III.—*Monuments which from their advanced stage of decay, or comparative unimportance, it is impossible or unnecessary to preserve.*

Wherever inscriptions are mentioned the word "inscription" is printed in Old English type to catch the eye and so help those who may be more especially interested in epigraphy to find them in the text.

At the end, at page 89, will be found a glossary of names and terms giving their meanings—especially of all such as are printed in italics in the body of the book.

HENRY COUSENS.

POONA:
30th September 1896.

CLASSIFIED LIST FOR CONSERVATION PURPOSES

OF REMAINS IN THE

CENTRAL PROVINCES AND BERÂR.

(For an explanation of the classes see Preface.)

CENTRAL PROVINCES.

CLASS I*a*.

District.	Locality.	Description.
Nâgpur	Nâgpur	Old sculptures and inscribed stones in the Museum.
Damoh	Nohta	Old sculptured temple.
Sâgar	Eran	Old sculptures and inscriptions.
Mandlâ	Râmnagar	Old inscription giving the genealogy of the Râjâs of Mandla.
Narsinghpur	Narsinghpur	Old sculptures in the public gardens.

CLASS I*b*.

District.	Locality.	Description.
Chândâ	Mârkandi	Old temples.
Jabalpur	Bherâghât	Images and circular corridor of old temple on the hill.
,,	Rûpnâth	Rock-cut inscription of Aśoka.
Nimar	Mândhâtâ	The old temple of Siddhanâtha on the hill.
Râipur	Râjîm	Two old inscription slabs.

CLASS II*a*.

District.	Locality.	Description.
Chândâ	Junona	Ancient tank and palace.
,,	Bhândak	Old Hindu bridge.
,,	,,	Buddhist cave in Vinjhâsan hill.
Jabalpur	Tigowa	Temple of Kankâli devî.
Damoh	Damoh	Sculptures on the bank of the Phuteria tank; old doorway of carved stone in the Deputy Commissioner's garden and inscription slabs there and in the *Kacheri*.
,,	Singorgaḍ	Old Fort.
Sâgar	Rahatgaḍ	Old Fort.
Seoni	Lakhnadon	Old sculptures.
Nimâr	Asîrgarh	Old temple and inscription slabs.
Betul	Shegaḍ	Fort and gateways.

Class IIa—*contd.*

District.	Locality.	Description.
Râipur . .	. Arang . .	. Old sculptures and inscription slabs.
,, . .	. Balod . .	. A sati pillar with three inscriptions.

Class IIb.

District.	Locality.	Description.
Nâgpur . .	. Adâsâ . .	. Old temple.
Chândâ . .	. Chândâ . .	. The Gond tombs.
,, . .	. Bhândak . .	. An old temple about 500 yards west of the village, also two colossal sculptures in an enclosure on the south of the village.
,, . .	. Bhatâla . .	. An ancient temple.
Jabalpur . .	. Bahuriband .	. A colossal Jaina statue under a banyan tree.
,, . .	. Chhota Deori .	. An inscribed pillar with characters of the 6th or 7th cent.
,, . .	. Karnapara .	. A colossal Varâha or boar.
,, . .	. Majholi . .	. A colossal Varâha or boar.
,, . .	. Tewar . .	. Old sculptures in the village.
Sâgâr . .	. Sâgâr . .	. Old sculptures in the garden of the artillery mess-house.
Nimar . .	. Burhânpur .	. The Bibi and Jami masjids.
,, . .	. Mândhâtâ . .	. Gateway and other remains on the hill.
Hoshangâbâd .	. Pachmarhi .	. Old caves.
Betul . .	. Bhesdehi . .	. Old temple.
Râipur . .	. Chipti . .	. Temples and inscriptions.
,, . .	. Deo Baloda .	. Old temple of Śiva.
,, . .	. Nârâyanpur .	. Old temples.
,, . .	. Râjîm . .	. Temple of Râjîvalochana.
Bilâspur . .	. Amarkantak .	. Karṇa Mandira temple.
,, . .	. Biramdeva .	. Old temple and inscription slabs.
,, . .	. Gotaura . .	. Old sculptures.
,, . .	. Janjgira . .	. Old Vaishṇava temple.
,, . .	. Junâshahr .	. Remains of old buildings.
,, . .	. Kotgaḍ . .	. Old inscription slabs.
,, . .	. Seorinârâyan .	. Temple of Nârâyaṇa.
Sambalpur .	. Arbhar . .	. Old temple of Kâlî and inscription slab.
,, . .	. Pujaripali .	. Inscription slab.
,, . .	. Saria . .	. Two old temples.
,, . .	. Boidyanâth .	. Inscription slabs.

BERÂR.

Class Ia.

District.	Locality.	Description.
Akolâ . .	. Narnâla . .	. Mahâkâlî gateway.
,, . .	. ,, . .	. The Shahanur gateway.

CLASS I*b*.

District.	Locality.	Description.
Buldânâ	Fatehkheldâ	An old masjid.
"	Lonâr	Old temple in the village.

CLASS II*a*.

District.	Locality.	Description.
Akolâ	Bâlâpur	Old Fort.
"	Narnâla	Old Fort and inscriptions.
Buldânâ	Amdâpur	A colossal statue.

CLASS II*b*.

District.	Locality.	Description.
Akolâ	Bârsi Tâkli	The temple of Kâlikâ devî.
Buldânâ	Anjani Khurd	Old unfinished masjid.
"	Chandol	Old temples.
"	Lonâr	Old "Hemâdpanti" temples.
"	Rohinkhedâ	Old Jami masjid.
"	Sâtgâon	"Hemâdpanti" temples.

CONTENTS.

CENTRAL PROVINCES.

BERÂR.

CORRECTIONS.

Page 22, *entry* 9, *for* Chichgaḍ *read* Kachargaḍ.
„ 25 „ 6, *for* Kohargas *read* Kohargaḍ.
„ 44 „ 12, *for* Chawal *read* Chhawal.
„ 46 „ 31, *for* Nâgjheri *read* Nâgjhiri.
„ 46 „ 32, *for* Padalda *read* Patalda.
„ 46 „ 42, *for* Talim Khera *read* Tarankhera.
„ 46 „ 43, *for* Thatgaḍ *read* Khatgaḍ.
„ 59 „ 9, *for* Chapra *read* Kopra.
„ 64 „ 9, *for* Jharial *read* Jural.
„ 64 „ 10, *for* Kuliajoie *read* Koilighogar.
„ 65 „ 1, *for* Boidyanâth *read* Baidyanâth.
„ 65 „ 4, *for* Nandapala *read* Nandapali.
„ 67 „ 6, *for* Râni Jharial *read* Rânipur.

Page 28, *entry* 12, Karanpara *should be* Karanpura, *30 miles from Murwárá Khâs.*
„ 30, „ 21, Suror *is in the Panna State about 15 miles from Murwárá Khâs. There is also a* Surora *about 20 miles due north of Jukahi Railway Station.*

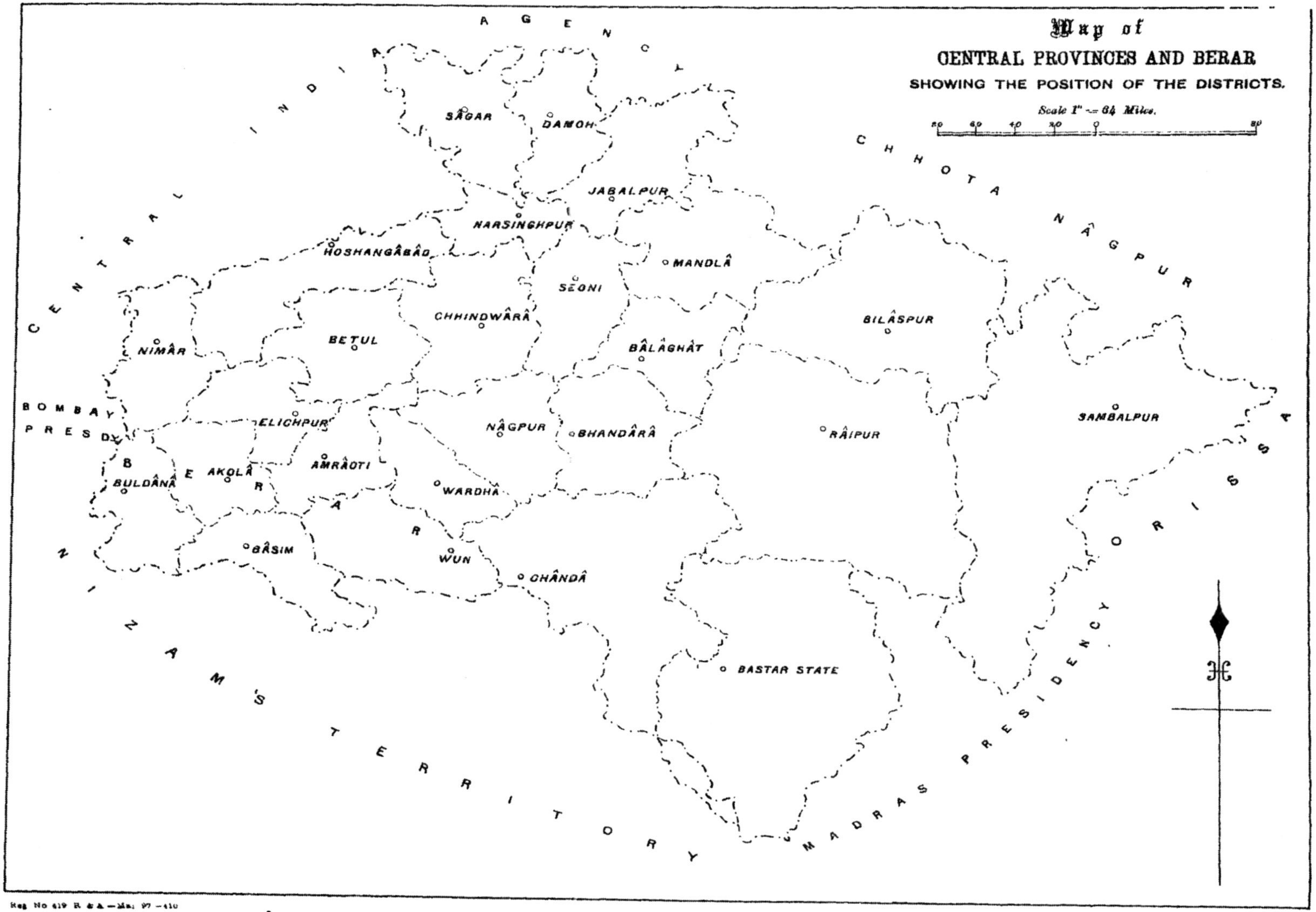

Reg. No 419 R. & A.—Mar. 97—410

Litho., S. I. O., Calcutta.

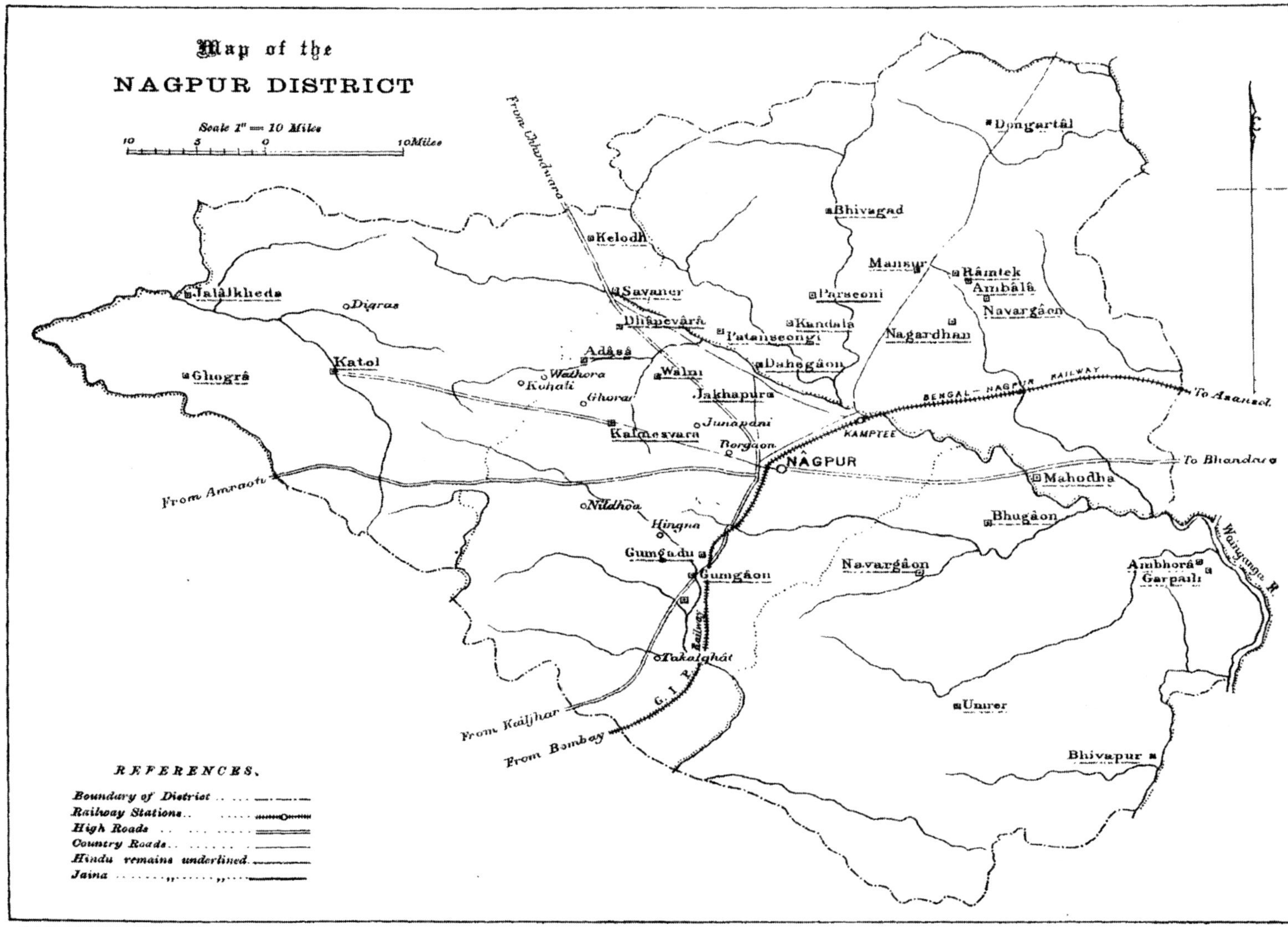
Map of the
NAGPUR DISTRICT
Scale 1" = 10 Miles
10 5 0 10Miles
Dongartâl
Bhivagad
Kelodh
Mansur
Râmtek
Ambâlâ
Navargâon
Jalâlkheda
Savaner
Parseoni
Digras
Dhâpevârâ
Kandala
Patanseongi
Nagardhan
Adâsâ
Katol
Dahegâon
Walni
Ghogrâ
Wathora
Kohali
Ghorai
Jakhapur
Junapani
Kalmesvara
Borgaon
KAMPTEE
NÂGPUR
BENGAL—NAGPUR RAILWAY
To Asansol
To Bhandara
From Chhindwara
From Amraoti
Mahodha
Nildhoa
Hingna
Bhugâon
Gumgadu
Gumgâon
Navargâon
Ambhorâ
Garpaili
Wainganga R.
Railway
Takalghât
G. I. P.
Umrer
From Kaljhar
From Bombay
Bhivapur
REFERENCES.
Boundary of District
Railway Stations
High Roads
Country Roads
Hindu remains underlined
Jaina ,, ,,

I.—NÂGPUR DIVISION.

I.—Nâgpur District.

Ia.† **1. Nâgpur.** The only remains of interest at Nâgpur itself are the sculptures and inscribed slabs which are gathered together in the museum. These have been collected from various quarters within the Central Provinces. From Bilhâri there are several well-carved pillars, a colossal head and bust of a *devi,** and a sculptured door-jamb; from Hoshangâbâd two Jaina and one other figure; from Mândhâtâ two large elephants and a large head of Śiva; from Khandwâ portions of Jaina figures; from Burhânpur some Jaina images and fragments; from Chândâ several figure sculptures. Seoni is represented by some well-cut images of Lakshmi-Nàrâyaṇa and Vishṇu; Mandlâ by a miscellaneous lot of figures including several *sati* stones; Sitâbaldi hill, Nâgpur, by a curiously carved slab containing an inscription and rows of small boars in relief, an old iron gun, and a *linga**; Bhandârâ by some images of sorts; Ratanpur by three door-jambs and other figures; and Bilâspur by a large figure of Brahmâ. In addition to the above there are some fragments not labelled, and some good, but late, wood carving. There are some Jaina and Hindu figures from Nimâr, Chicholi, Bâghnadi, and Lânji, and five heavy sandstone sarcophagi from Sironcha.

Inscriptions.—There are thirteen slabs bearing inscriptions, labelled as having come from Amarakantak, Jabalpur, Bilhâri, Râipur, Ratanpur, Lânji, and Chândâ. Impressions have been taken off all of these, and some of them have been published with translations in the Journals of the Bombay Branch of the Royal Asiatic Society for 1842 and 1843, in the XVIIth volume of General Cunningham's Reports, and in Parts I and V of the first, IX and XII of the second, and VII of the third volumes of *Epigraphia Indica.*

IIb.† **2. Adásá,** 18 miles north-west of Nàgpur, and connected with that place by a country track. Here are five old temples and two tanks. This part of the country was in old times called "Vidarbhadeśa," and the present locality "Adàsâ Kshetra."

(1) The temple of Gaṇapati contains an image of Vakratuṇḍa or Gaṇapati, made of a single stone so set up that worshippers may walk around it. There is said to be beneath it a small image made of Kâshmiri stone which is believed to have been set up by the god Indra. The temple is said to have been built over the image by the famous Hemâdpant. The present *sabhā maṇḍapa** is reported to have been built by Sambhâji Bunbâji, son of Râghoji I, ruler of Nâgpur, in the *Fasli* year 1181. Gosâvis are the attached worshippers, who worship in the morning, offer their presents at noon, and close the doors of the temple in the evening after making the

* For explanation of these terms see Glossary at end.

† For description of classes for conservation purposes see Appendix.

arti (presenting lights). The temple is, on the whole, in good order, and is maintained by a Government grant of money and some land. It is in the custody of the *málguzárs* of Adâsâ. There is a cell behind the mountain. In this cell Bagâji Bhure, a devotee, is said to have performed his austerities about a century ago. This Bagâji fixed the localities of the different *tírthas* mentioned below :—

Cherum Tîrtha, a well in the town.
Oṁkâra Tîrtha, the *paka* built tank now existing.
Gaṇeśa Tîrtha, the small puddle near the tank.
Mûshaka Tîrtha, the *bávali* with the built steps.
Ikshu Sâgara, the small tank at the place.
Bindu Tîrtha, the ditch on the mountain.
Madhu Sudhâ, the rivulet towards Dhâpevârâ road.
Pâpavimochana Tîrtha, the rivulet towards the Khapa road.

(2) The temple of Mahâdeva stands on the hill and is also ascribed to Hemâdpant. The three *lingas*, which are collectively called Tryambakeśvara, are believed to have sprung up from the earth spontaneously. The temple is of stone, and is in the custody of the *mâlguzârs* of Adâsâ.

The temples of (3) Mâruti, (4) Ambikâ, and (5) Kâla Bhairava do not appear to be of much account, except in that a part of, or an incomplete Hemâdpanti temple stands on the *chabutrá* of the latter.

The old tank of Oṁkâra Tîrtha was built of stone masonry by a son of Râghoji I. The southern and northern sides fell into decay, but they were afterwards restored by the Marâthâ Queen Bakâ Bâi of Nâgpur. The northern side is again crumbling. The small tank of Ganeśa Kuṇḍa is also one of the eight *tírthas*. Its banks were rebuilt by the Bhonsle rulers about forty years ago. Jani Bâi, the Nâtakśâlâ of Râghoji III. built a *mundali* (wall) of bricks, which is still in existence.

III. 3. **Ambálá**, a tank a mile and a half east of Râmtek and about 28 miles north-east of Nâgpur. Tradition traces the origin of this tank as far back as the *Tretá Yuga*. One Amba Râjâ bathed in this tank while out hunting, and was thereby completely cured of a troublesome skin disease. In gratitude he enlarged the tank and built the *ghâts* which lead down to the water. Standing around the tank are the following buildings :—(1) A palace said to have been built by a Sûrya Vamsi ruler, with hewn stones and mortar, on the north of the tank. (2) Panchakalasi Banglâ, a sort of bastion with five domes, built of hewn stones and mortar. (3) A temple of 32 pillars, built by the Marâthâs. (4) A large gate towards the south. (5) A temple dedicated to Sûrya Nârâyaṇa. (6) A temple to Mahâdeva. (7) The *ghâts* built previous to, but repaired by, the Bhonsles. In addition to these, several temples have been built by the families of Bhalarav, Jamdar, and others. The tank is in good repair, but is not in the custody of any one.

III. 4. **Ambhorá**, 35 miles east-south-east of Nâgpur and 10 miles south of Bhandârâ, on the Wainganga river. There is here a temple of Chaitanyeśvara, said to be a Hindu one and built by Hemâdpant. Fairs are held here on the Hindu festival days of *Mahá Śivarâtri* and on other particular holy days, when pilgrims attend from Nâgpur, Bhandârâ, Umrer, and other places. There is a grant of R100 per annum from the District Fund for the repair of the road from the village to the hill. One Antobâ Kalar of Nâgpur has repaired the temple thoroughly. Here is also the *samâdha* of Har Har Svâmi, where a hall was built by the Bhonsle Râjâs of Nâgpur of wood and stones with mortar. Its surrounding walls were repaired by Nânâ Sâheb Chitnavis. There are steps built for ascending the hill towards the temple. More recently repaired by Antobâ Kalar and others of Nâgpur.

III. 5. **Bhivagaḍ,** 18 miles to the north of Nâgpur. Close to the Pench river, on the top of a very steep hill, are the remains of this fort. The top of the hill is encircled with walls made of ponderous masses of rock. The lines of defence, especially over the pathway leading up the hillside, are constructed with some skill. The work is evidently very ancient, and is referred by the people to the "Gavalis."

III. 6. **Bhivapur,** a town 16 miles south-east of Umrer and 44 from Nâgpur. It was a very early settlement of the Gonds, the original settler having been one Bhimsa, who in the middle of the 16th century built the now dilapidated fort as a protection to his little colony. Here are numerous *sati* monuments in the shape of pillars, both squared and rough, slabs, and rude monoliths. One slab, measuring 10 feet high and 5 feet broad, is set up on a *chabutrá* in the market place, and is now worshipped with copious libations of sour milk, oil, and vermillion. Close to it stands a square *dîpadâna* or pillar. On the crest of the embankment of the tank are several *sati* stones, the shelving banks on the city sides having numerous little *sati chabutrâs* and temples. At the north-east end of the city are the ruins of the fort. (*See* General Cunningham's Vol. VII., p. 121.)

III. 7. **Bhugáon,** 16 miles north of Umrer and 14 miles south-east of Nâgpur. An old temple of Mahâdeva and a tank called Pushkariṇi, constructed of great blocks of stones without mortar, not sculptured, and ascribed to Hemâdpant. The temple is in a good state of preservation, but the tank has fallen out of repair.

III. 8. **Borgáon,** 4 miles west of Nâgpur; in the neighbourhood are some old stone circles similar to those at Junapani. They are said to be of Scythian origin.

III. 9. **Dahegáon,** 12 miles north of Nâgpur, a tank built by Bakâ Bâi at a cost of about R10,000. The Nâgpur Râjâ performed a ceremony in honour of the tank in the *Fasli* year 1249, on his return from Benâres. It belongs to the Bhonsle estate.

III. 10. **Dhápevárá,** 24 miles north-west of Nâgpur. Temple of Vithobâ, also a fort which was built for protection against the Pindâris. The image enshrined in the temple is said to have arisen spontaneously under the boughs of a *banyan* rooted in the sand of the river on the bank of which stands the temple. One Umarji Abâ, who was in the service of the Nâgpur Râjâs, got the temple erected over this idol about 125 years ago, in obedience to a divine injunction. Afterwards one Timaji Pant *alias* Bâpuji Brâhman, built the present hall (*sabhâ maṇḍapa*) and the car (*ratha*) about 80 years ago. The northern and southern sides of the temple were in ruins when Muratsinha Jamâdâr re-built them at his own expense in 1252 *Fasli.* He also built the front temples of Puṇḍalîka and Mâruti, together with the *ghât* of the river, about 60 years ago. This *ghât* is now out of repair. The old hall of the temple was renewed by Govind Sinha Jamâdâr in 1275 *Fasli.* The temple is now in good order and is supported by Government grant or *nemnûk.* The worship and other ceremonies connected with this temple are regularly performed. A *Purâṇîka* attached to the temple also gets a *nemnûk* pension. In the months of Kârtika and Âshâdha fairs are held, when the car is moved with great pomp.

III. 11. **Digras.** Between Digras and Sàvargâon are a number of stone circles covering an area of about 3 miles.

III. 12. **Dongartál,** about two miles to the west of the present metalled road, midway between Seoni and Nâgpur. Possesses a locally sacred tank, the ruins of a small fort, probably modern, and a small **inscription** of two lines on the rock. The inscription is in modern characters and seems to be the record of a pilgrim. There is nothing of interest in the place. (General Cunningham's Reports, Vol. VII., p. 109.)

III. 13. **Garpaili.** Near the village there is a hill known as Kola Surav Pahâd in which are four caves. In one of them is the image of Mahâdeva (Śiva). No one worships there regularly, but some people go and offer their prayers, etc., on the Hindu holiday called *Śivarâtri.* A temple built by Antobâ Kalar of Nagpur.

III. 14. **Ghográ** and Savaga. These are very curious old buildings. The stones used are very massive and the carving good. No cement of any kind is to be traced. They consist of a centre room with a dome formed with considerable skill, a portico in front and two little rooms on each side of the centre room. These and all the other temples above named, made without cement, are referred by the people to the work of the *Ṛishis.* They are certainly very old, but they appear to be Hindu and not Buddhist. This belief is strengthened by the existence of a very distinct carving of Gaṇeśa in the centre of the Savaga temple.

III. 15. **Ghorar** and Kohali, 15 and 20 miles north-west of Nâgpur, stone circles covering a very great area about the villages Khapri and Ubji between Ghorar and Kohali.

III. 16. **Gumgadu,** 10 miles south-west of Nâgpur. The temple of Mahâdeva erected by Râṇi Bakâ Bâi, grand-mother of Râghoji III, about the *Fasli* year 1216. The building is said to have cost her about R5,000. The village was a *mokása* to Râṇi Daryâ Bâi, who maintained the temple.

III. 17. **Gumgáon,** a small village, 12 miles south of Nâgpur, has an old fort of considerable size, and a well-built temple of Gaṇapati.

III. 18. **Hingna,** 10 miles south-west of Nâgpur. Formerly there was an army encampment in the neighbourhood of Hingna, and large stones are here and there set up. There are two heaps of stones on the way to Nâgpur.

III. 19. **Jakhapur,** 7 miles north of Nâgpur on the Savaner road, an old temple of Kâli, constructed of great blocks of stone without mortar, but not decorated. It is in a good state of preservation. It is surrounded by an enclosure of brickwork built recently. The *sabhá mandapa* is also of recent date, having been built by a concubine of the Nâgpur Râjâ. The shrine is 17′×16′, the *sabhá mandapa* 23′×21′, and the enclosure 114′×70′. A fair is held here annually on the 15 Chaitra in honour of the *devi.* There are a few *inám* fields for the maintenance of the temple. The building is ascribed to Hemâdpant.

III. 20. **Jaláikheda,** situated about 14 miles west of Kâtol. The remains of a large fort ascribed to the Gavali Râjâs, and for nearly 2 miles around the present village are traces of the old town.

III. 21. **Junapani,** 9 miles west of Nâgpur. In the neighbourhood are numbers of stone circles. These circles are of great age. No one can now say exactly what they are, but it is commonly believed that they mark the site of temporary encampments of the Gavalis, or pastoral tribes who wandered from place to place with their cattle. Others say that such places were formerly used for interring dead bodies. Sometimes iron nails and tools are found beneath the stones. Possibly they are of Scythian origin.

III. 22. **Kalmeśvara,** 14 miles west of Nâgpur. In the centre of the town, on elevated ground, is an old fortress. It is said to have been built by a Hindu family from Delhi, which, in the time of Bakht Buland, the Gond râjâ of Deogaḍ, maintained for the royal service a force of 400 infantry and 100 cavalry.

III. 23. **Kandala,** 13 miles north-west of Nâgpur. An old temple said to have been built by Hemâdpant.

III. 24. **Katol,** 36 miles north-west of Nâgpur. The remains of an old fort are still to be seen overhanging the river banks. There is a curious temple here of very early date, built entirely of layers of sandstone, which must have been quarried many miles off. No mortar is used about it and the stones have many grotesque carvings. It is called the house of Bhavâni, but is without an image or any legend, save that of an undefined miraculous origin. This part of the country is said to be the ancient Kuntalapura, the ruler of which was Chandrahâsya, a contemporary of Durbuddhi Pradhâna mentioned in the *Purâṇas.*

III. 25. **Kelodh,** 30 miles north-west of Nâgpur. The temple of the Kalavantin supposed to be one of the 360 temples built by Hemâdpant. It was for some time occupied by a *kalavantin* or concubine.

The temple portion no longer exists; there is only a *sabhá maṇḍapa* or hall, and even this is falling into decay.

On one of the stones is an **inscription** in a character like *Bâlabodha*, which has not yet been deciphered. Local tradition assigns it to the *kalavantin.* She is said to have hidden her treasures under it, and to have given orders that no one but a relative should remove the stone. There are signs of an attempt having been made to raise it, but by whom and with what success is not known. (2) Also a ruined fort.

III. 26. **Mahodha,** 21 miles east of Nâgpur, has a very curious *sati* stone, on the face of which is a very rudely carved female figure, standing to the front, and holding a club in her left hand. (Cunningham's Reports, Vol. XVII., p. 1.)

III. 27. **Mansur,** 24 miles north-east of Nâgpur. Hill and temple of Hidimbâ. This *pahâd* (hill) has the tradition that some centuries ago a great female demon, by name Hidimbâ, used to live on it, in a palace built by herself. The existing tank is also said to be of her creation. About a century ago every traveller who happened to halt here could get, it is said, out of the tank all the utensils required for cooking himself a meal. The only condition imposed on the traveller was that he should restore them to the tank when he had done with them. Once upon a time a traveller who had had the use of the utensils appropriated them out of covetousness. No sooner was this solemn condition broken than the supply of cooking utensils ceased. The temple does not now exist. Also a temple to the god "Mânbhau" where an annual *jâtra* is held in the month of Chaitra.

28. **Nagardhan,** 4 miles south of Râmtek; a temple dedicated to Koteśvara, and an old ruined fort.

29. **Navargáon,** 2 miles south-east of Ambâlâ tank. On a *pahâd,* or hill, within the limits of the village, but close to Ambâlâ tank, is a temple with a *sabhá maṇḍapa* dedicated to Nâgârjuna.

III. 30. **Nildhoa,** 16 miles west of Nâgpur. Stone circles.

III. 31. **Parseoni,** 16 miles north of Nâgpur. A Jaina temple and remains of a fort.

This temple is built of white stone, and the image is of a white marble. The worshippers are Jains and Mârvâdis. The temple is in fair condition.

The remains of the fort are situated on the top of a very steep hill close by the Pench river. The top of the hill is fenced round with walls made of ponderous masses of rock.

The lines of defence, especially over the pathway leading up the hill side, are constructed with some skill. The work is evidently very ancient indeed, and is referred by the people to the "Gavalis."

III. 32. **Patanseongi,** 16 miles north-west of Nâgpur. This place is of considerable antiquity. Traditions in the "Svasthânik" (Gond Râjâs') family tell how in A. D. 1742, in the struggle between Wali Shâh and the legitimate princess, 12,000 men were massacred by the victorious party in and round the now ruined fort. It continued to be the station of a troop of horse up to the decease of the late Râjâ; until lately it was the head-quarters of a *tehśil.*

33. **Râmtek,** 28 miles north-east of Nâgpur. The following are its remains and legends :—

In the Satya *Yuga* the district was covered with dense forest, and the hill was then known under the name of "Tapogiri" (mountain of devotion or austerity).

Afterwards, in the same *Yuga*, when the god Narasinha, an incarnation of Vishṇu, killed Hiraṇya Kaśipu, the hill acquired the name Sindûragiri, from the streams of blood that issued from the monster. On this mountain Agastya Ṛishi performed his *tapah* (devotion or austerity).

In the reign of Râma, a Brâhmaṇ, inconsolable for the death of his son at the early age of 500 years (for the limit of life was then fixed at 1,000 years) took the corpse to Râma Râjâ, and ascribed the untimely death to the sins of the hero's kingdom. Then Râma asked his priest, by name Vasishṭha Ṛishi, to tell him what he knew of the cause. The priest replied that a Sûdra had begun to practise austerities on the Sindûragiri. (This is a sin in Śûdras according to the *Śâstras.*) Râma with his brother Lakshmaṇa went to this spot and found the Śûdra making a *dharmapa* at the foot of the Sindûragiri. Râma pierced him with an arrow and he fainted away saying "Râma" "Râma." No sooner did Râma hear this dying cry than he approached him, and, in remorse, assured him of the restoration of his life, and offered him anything that he might ask. But the dying Śûdra was happy to die in Râma's presence and only begged that they two—Râma and Lakshmaṇa—should remain where they were to the end of the world, and that his body should be turned into a *piṇḍi* (the form in which the god Śiva is worshipped). The request was readily granted, and the body of the Śûdra was changed into a stone *piṇḍi*, with the name of Dharmeśvara. One Benirain Dani is said to have built the present temple over the *piṇḍi*.

Râma restored the Brâhmaṇ's son to life, went back to Ayodhyâ with all his attendants, made over the sovereign authority to his sons and returned to the Sindûragiri to fulfil the promise given to the dying Śûdra. Since his settling on this hill it has been called Râmakshetra (Râma's field) or Râmatekdi (Râma's hill).

Afterwards one Hemâdpant (some say a Râkshasa, and others a Brâhmaṇ) built the following five temples on the Râmtek hill :—

(1) Temple dedicated to Râma, built of a kind of silicious stone, commonly known among the Hindus as "Râṅgoḷi" stone, containing images of Râma and Sîtâ.
(2) Temple of Lakshmaṇasvâmi built of the same kind of stone.
(3) Hanumân's temple.
(4) A temple dedicated to the goddess "Ekâdaśi."
(5) Temple of Lakshmi-Nârâyaṇa.
(6) Temple of Dhûmreśvara Mahâdeva.
(7) "A *dharamaśâlâ.*"
(8) "Gokula Darvâzâ."

All these buildings are massive and elegant.

The Sûrya Vamśi Kings (Solar race), who are said to have founded the town of

Râmtek, are credited with adding the following buildings to those already enumerated as situated on the hill of Râmtek :—

(1) Râma Jharukâ.
(2) Royal Palace.
(3) Temple dedicated to Venkateśa (Lakshmi-Nârâyana).
(4) Rampart around the fortress built with hewn stones and mortar.
(5) Bhairava Darvâzâ (gate).
(6) "Singhpur" gate.
(7) "Varâha" gate.
(8) Temple dedicated to Daśaratha.
(9) A large tank.
(10) Temple built over the image of "Varâha." The image is said to have been in existence since the Tretâ *Yuga*.
(11) Two temples dedicated to the god Narasinha.

Then followed the Gond kings whose names are not connected with any buildings, except the wall round the fort with two gates known as Parvara gates. Next to these come the Bhonsle Rulers. The following works are assigned to them.

Two flights of stairs, one from the Ambâlâ tank to the *gaḍ*, *viz.*, the citadel where the several temples above specified cluster, and the other from the citadel, towards the town of Râmtek.

The well called Sindûra *bávali* is said to have come into existence in the following way. After Narasinha killed the monster Hiraṇya Kaśipu, he threw away his cudgel on the mountain. The impact was so terrible as to make a hole large enough for the *bávali*.

This sacred well has been, according to the above tradition, in existence since the Tretâ *Yuga*. But its stone building and the adjoining *dharmaśálá* are said to be the hand-work of the famous Hemâdpant.

Of the origin of the images of Bahiṇa-Bhâu there is the following tradition:—

Once upon a time there lived a brother and a sister, the latter serving the former. On one occasion the brother got angry and killed her. They both then came to Agastya Ṛishi for redress. The Ṛishi consoled them by foretelling the redress of their grievance on Râma's advent; and they returned to their home and remained there for ever. (*See* General Cunningham's Reports, Vol. VII., p. 109 *et seq.*)

III. 34. **Savaner,** 23 miles to the north-west of Nâgpur, reached by a good made road, the old temple of Mahâdeva, constructed of great blocks of stones without mortar, and ascribed to Hemâdpant. Also the ruins of a well-planned fort supposed to be of Gavali origin. The temple has an income of R10 annually.

III. 35. **Takalghát,** 10 miles south-west of Nâgpur. Mounds around the village, and rough stone circles covering five and a half acres, about a mile distant, from which have been dug fragments of pottery, flint arrow heads, and iron ware, evidently of great antiquity.

III. 36. **Umrer,** 28 miles south-east of Nâgpur. A Maráthâ fort and an old temple. (Cunningham's Reports, Vol. VII., p. 118.)

III. 37. **Walni,** 14 miles north-west of Nâgpur. An old temple ascribed to Hemâdpant.

III. 38. **Wathora,** 20 miles north-west of Nâgpur. Stone circles known as *chabutrâs* of the Gavalis. It is stated that some two centuries ago a Gavali king reigned over a tract between the Godâvari and Narmadâ. The Gavalis were pasturing tribes who used to wander from place to place with their cattle, halting where fodder was plentiful and seeking better pastures when they felt a scarcity impending. These circles are said to be the remains of their temporary encampments.

II.—Wardhâ.

III. 1. **Arvi,** 34 miles north-west of Wardhâ. The town is said to have been founded about 300 years ago by Telang Râv. Hindus claim him as a Brâhmaṇ, the Muhammadans as a Muhammadan, and both worship at his tomb.

III. 2. **Ashti,** 52 miles north-west of Wardhâ, the mausoleums of Muhammad Khân and Ahmad Khân Niazi. The Emperor Jahangir gave the Ashti *parganá* in *jágir* to Muhammad Khân Niazi, an Afghân noble of high rank and repute. He died at Ashti in 1037 *Fasli* and was buried there, and a handsome mausoleum was built over his grave. Ahmad Khân Niazi succeeded him, and after a rule of 14 years died at Ashti in 1061 *Fasli*: a similar mausoleum was built over his tomb. The two stand side by side within an enclosure. Also the remains of an old Marâthâ fort.

III. 3. **Bhiri,** 18 miles west of Wardhâ, a sculptured temple of Gopâla Deva which is in good repair. There are two *mokása* villages, the profits of which are devoted to the support of the temple.

III. 4. **Birul,** 19 miles west of Wardhâ, a mud fort which is ruined.

III. 5. **Devalvádá,** a fine temple of Rukmi.

III. 6. **Girar,** 37 miles east of Wardhâ, shrine of Khwâja Farid. This saint was born in Hindusthân and at last settled on the Girar hill. The Zeolitic concretions on the Girar hill are said to be the petrified cocoanuts and other articles of merchandise belonging to travelling traders who mocked the saint, on which he turned their whole stock in trade into stones as a punishment. They implored his pardon; and he created a fresh stock for them from dry leaves.

III. 7. **Keljhar,** 17 miles north-east of Wardhâ, an old fort, and a temple of Gaṇapati. Keljhar is said to occupy the site of an ancient city called Chakrangar, an account of which, and of the demon which preyed upon it, is to be found in the *Mahábhárata*.

III. 8. **Náchangáon,** 21 miles south-west of Wardhâ, a fort which was successfully used by the inhabitants for purposes of self-defence against the Pindâris. A carved stone in the wall which is in the middle of the fort purports to show that the building was constructed four centuries ago by one Dad Shâh Lar.

III. 9. **Paunar,** 5 miles north-east of Wardhâ, a fort and *masjid*. The fort appears to have been a place of considerable strength. The ruins of the old town wall are still traceable, and one of the gateways, a large imposing structure of stone, yet remains. There is an inscription in what appears to be the *Devanágari* character upon the gateway.

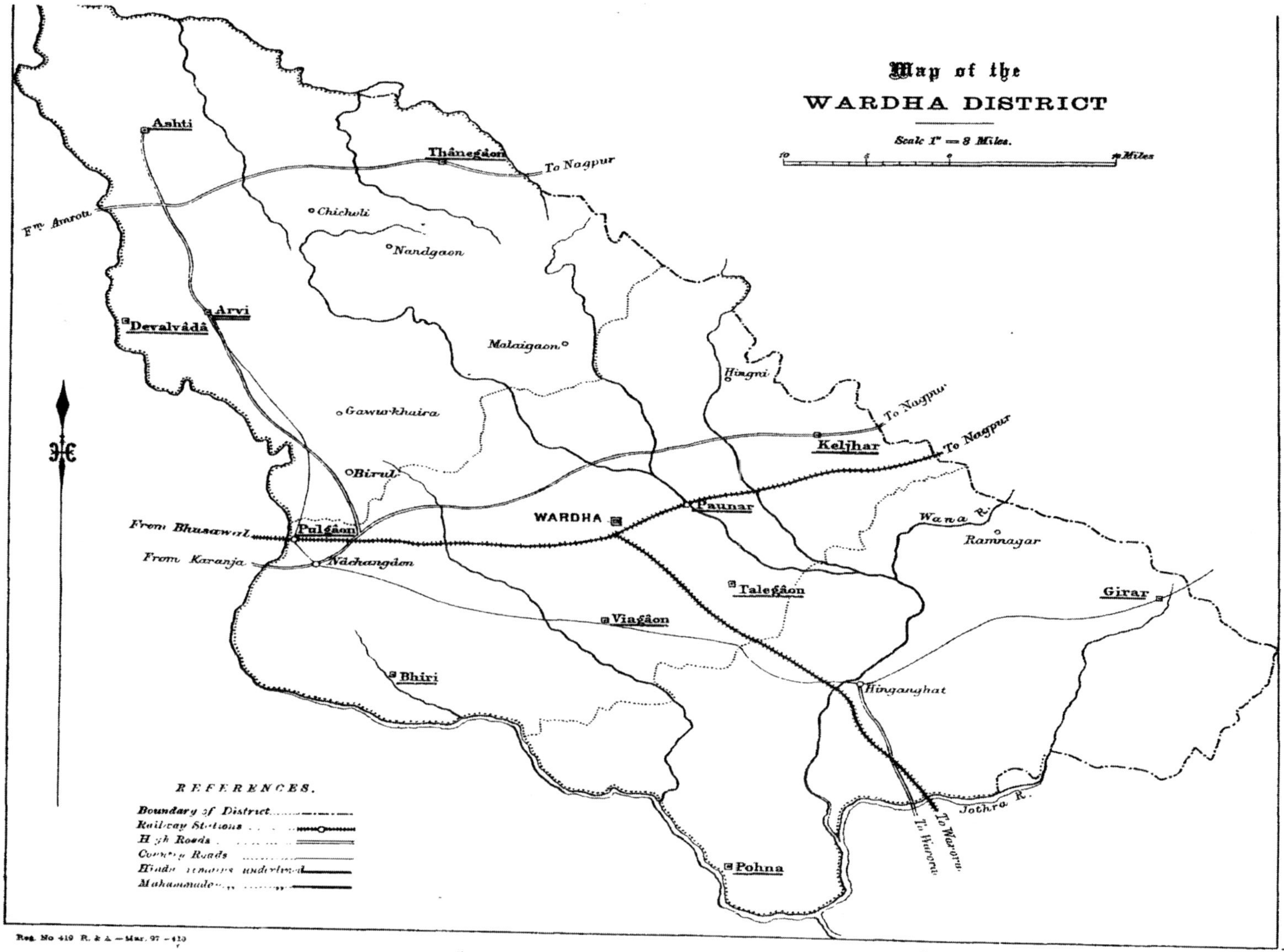

Reg. No 419 R. & A.—Mar. 97—410

Litho., S. I. O. Calcutta

III. · 10. **Pohna,** on the Wardhâ river and about 16 miles south-west of Hinganghât, a temple of Rudreśvara, constructed of stone and mortar, and said by some to have been built by Râjâ Pratâb Rudra. Others ascribe it to Hemâdpant. It is in ruins, but its repair is about to be undertaken.

III. ·11. **Pulgáon,** 21 miles west of Wardhâ, temple of Mahâdeva.

III. , 12. **Rhoni,** a fine temple of Koteśvara, on the banks of the Wardhâ, about 20 miles south-west from Wardhâ, constructed of great blocks of stone with mortar, and in good repair.

III. 13. **Talegáon,** about 10 miles south of Wardhâ and 2 miles from Sonegâon railway station. Temple of Mahâdeva in a dilapidated state and very old. It is ascribed to Hemâdpant. Also a temple of Devi. There is said to be a very old "*chauk*" buried 8 feet under the house of one Sambhâppâ Desmukh.

III. 14. **Thánegáon,** about 26 miles north-east of Arvi, the temple of Devi, said to have been erected in the *Śâlivâhan* era 1145 or A.D. 1223 as appears from a long unintelligible **inscription,** where the figures only can be read. The temple is not of much architectural merit and is in good repair.

III. 15. **Viagáon,** an old temple of Bâlâji, of much local repute, where a *jatrá* is held.

III.—Chândâ District.

III. **1. Chándá.** Chândâ is a large walled town situated in the fork between the Jharpat *nálá* and the Erai river. It is about one mile and a half in length, by a mile and a quarter in breadth, but the greater part of the enclosed space is vacant. The walls were built by the Gond Râjâ Khândkia Ballâl Shâh, the contemporary of Akbar; but they were repaired by the Marâthâs and are now in excellent order. The walls are rather low, with lofty battlements, and they form a very efficient protection against the flood waters of the Erai river when driven backwards by the inundation of the Wardhâ river.

The only buildings of any consequence are some temples and the tombs of the later Gond kings, the last are plain and substantial buildings, but rather heavy in appearance. The gateways offer good specimens of Gond art, as they are ornamented with sculptures of the fabulous monster lion overpowering an elephant, which was the symbol of the Gond kings.

The temples are generally plâin with pyramidal roofs in steps, the only exception is the fane of Achaleśvara, the walls of which are covered with a multitude of small sculptured panels. There are several sculptures of the Nâga, but only one of them is of large size, with two smaller snakes on the same slab.

III. Outside the town to the south-east, at a picturesque spot called Lâlpet, there is a large collection of colossal figures which are more remarkable for their size than for their artistic excellence. They lie upon the ground in various positions, and would appear to have been quarried and carved on the spot. The largest of them measures 26 feet × 18 feet × 3 feet. (Cunningham's Report, Vol. IX., p. 136.)

The popular legend is that there lived in the reign of Dhundiramsha, a wealthy Komti, by name Râyâppâ, who conceived the idea of doing some memorable act. He accordingly got these monoliths cut intending to place them in a temple of Śiva. But he died before he could build the temple, and the monoliths are lying as he left them. They are known as Râyâppâ's idols.

Between the town and these monoliths is a well, in the interior of which are built in some rather good sculptured stones.

The following are some of the traditions regarding the Chândâ temples :—

(1) The temple of Mahâkâli.

The Brahminical legends are that during the Krita *Yuga* the city of Lokâpura
III. extended over a wide expanse, including the site where now stands the modern town of Chândâ. Here resided the goddess Mahâkâli, and here she created a son, the beautiful Bhûtanâtha. The gods, however, enraged at his intrigues with their wives complained to Mahâkâli, who changed his name from Bhûtanâtha to Achaleśvara (the immovable), and sealing him with the print of a cow's hoof, fixed him for ever on the banks of the Jharpat.

The modern account of the temple is that when Ballâlshâh was reigning in 1262 at Junona, the capital of his kingdom, he was cured of his bodily disease by the use of the water accumulated in the cow's hoof marks on Achaleśvara. He had therefore much reverence for the place. Once he dreamed that to the south-eastern side of Achaleśvara, at a small distance, the goddess Mahâkâli had been buried under ground for a long time; and that he was asked to explore the underground chamber. He did so, and sanctioned a *nemnûk* grant and appointed a *pujâri.*

Afterwards Ballâlshâh's daughter-in-law, Hirâbâi, built the temple of Mahâkâli, about 500 years ago.

In 1647, Birsha ascended the throne. He had a beautiful daughter, who was given in marriage to Durgapâla, the son of the king of Devagaḍ. Learning subsequently that Durgapâla had spoken insultingly to the princess, he vowed to Mahâkâli that if victory were given him he would offer Durgapâla's head at her shrine * * * In the battle which ensued, Birsha was on the point of being captured, when unsheathing the sacred sword of his house he rushed at Durgapâla, and with the cry of "Victory to Mahàkâli" severed the prince's head from his shoulders. He took the head to Chândâ, and offered it in fulfilment of his vow.

His wife Hirâbâi pulled down the old temple of Mahâkâli and erected a new one on its site, and on the spire looking towards Nâgpur she fixed a stone bust of the slain Durgapâla, which is still to be seen there.

III. (2) The temple of Achaleśvara.

Achaleṣvara was formerly known as Jharpateśvara, which name was given to him by Reṇukâ, the goddess of Mehur (see *Skanda Purâṇa*).

The temple of Achaleśvara was built by Hirâbâi, the daughter-in-law of Ballâlshâh, between 1342 to 1382 A.D.

Afterwards, in the year 1790, Vyankâji *alias* Nânâ Sâheb pulled down the old temple and built the present one.

III. (3) The temple of Ekniri. The Purânic account is that on one occasion Achaleśvara had got angry with his mother Mahâkâli and had gone away to Reṇukâ, the goddess of Mâtâpur. Mahâkâli therefore went to get him back, and with him returned Reṇukâ, who is known here as Ekniri.

The present temple was built by Hirâbâi. The *sabhâ maṇḍapa* in front of the temple was built by Sankrâji Pant, *Subhedâr* of Chândâ, in 1808.

III. (4) The temple of Someśvara. This temple was built by Hirsha, the tenth Gond king. The popular account is that his queens used to come here for worship. When Mr. Crawford was Superintendent he pulled down the outer ramparts of the Ballâlkillâ. Consequently the temple is now outside the Ballâlkillâ.

III. (5) The temple of Gaṇpati was said to have been on the eastern gate of the ancient city of Bhadrâvati.

Hirâbâi built a temple in honour of Gaṇpati. Afterwards between 1780 and 1790, one Baba Bâi Khatni performed *sati*, and the present temple is said to have been built by her descendants by spending her money. The present Gaṇapati's temple is consequently known as Khatni's Gaṇpati temple.

III. (6) Jod Deval. This temple, built by Hirâbâi, is remarkable for a *linga* of Mahâdeva placed on an elephant. There is also an image of Keśavanâtha.

III. (7) Temple of Mâruti. The popular legend is that this Mâruti has been there since the time when the ancient city of Bhadrâvati existed. The present temple was built by one Râyâppâ Komti about 300 years ago in the reign of Dhundirâmsha.

II*b*. The Gond tombs are eight in number, and belong to the following kings and queens:—

(1) Hirsha, the 11th Gond king.
(2) Hirâi, the queen of Hirsha.
(3) Bâlâji Ballâlshâh, the 14th Gond king.
(4) Dhundirâmshâh, the 15th Gond king.
(5) Gangâbâi, the wife of Krishnasha, the 16th Gond king.
(6) Birsha, the 17th Gond king. This is the highest and best tomb.
(7) Nibonibhya Ballâlshâh, the son of Nilkanthshâh.
(8) Kodya Ballâlshâh.

III. There is also a well said to be in the form of a *śankha*.

This is an old well and is remarkable on account of its construction in the shape of a conch shell (*śankha*). In the reservoir there is a temple of Panchâyatana. It was built by one Bâpuji Vaidya, the Divâṇ of Hirâbâi, or by one of his predecessors, about 500 years ago.

III. 2. **Adial**, probably "Adyallee," 8 miles south by west of Châmursi; a fine irregular reservoir.

III. 3. **Amgáon**, 22 miles to the south-east of Mul, a temple in the Hemâdpant style.

III. 4. **Armori**, 58 miles north-east of Chândâ. An old triple-shrined Śaiva temple ascribed to Râjâ Hara Chandra Gond, situated upon a high mound called the *killá*. Other fragments and sculptures lying about point to the probability of there having been more temples than this at one time. A large embanked tank to the north-west of the temple adds much to its beauty; on its banks at the further end are a few cut-stone fragments. (Cunningham's Reports, Vol. VII., p. 125.)

III. 5. **Ballálpur**, a village in the Chândâ district, 6 miles south of Chândâ on the Wardhâ river. There is a fine stone fort, much of which is modern, having been rebuilt about the end of the last century. Within it are the remains of the ancient palace, among which are two tunnels sloping at a steep angle into the ground. The entrances are a few feet apart, and the tunnels, branching off in opposite directions, lead each to a set of three underground chambers. When these were explored in A.D. 1865, some ancient copper coins and decayed iron rings were found. There is also a perpendicular shaft, the object of which has not yet been ascertained. North of the village are the ruins of a large and elaborately made tank, in which, owing probably to the falling in of the under-channels, any water collected sinks through the earth, and appears as a stream a little further down. To the east stands a tomb of one

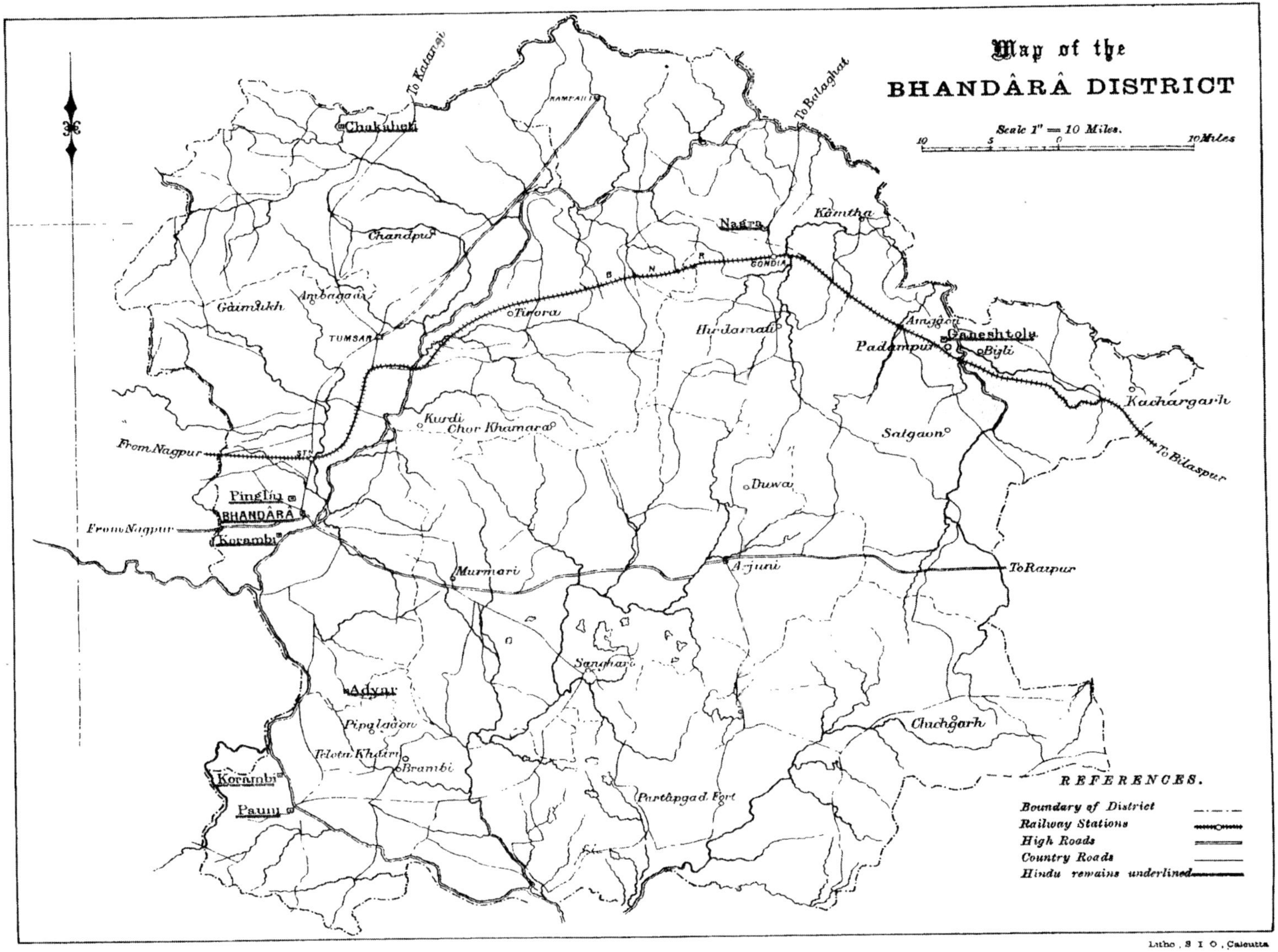

Litho, S I O, Calcutta

Reg. No 419 R & A.—Jan 97 –410

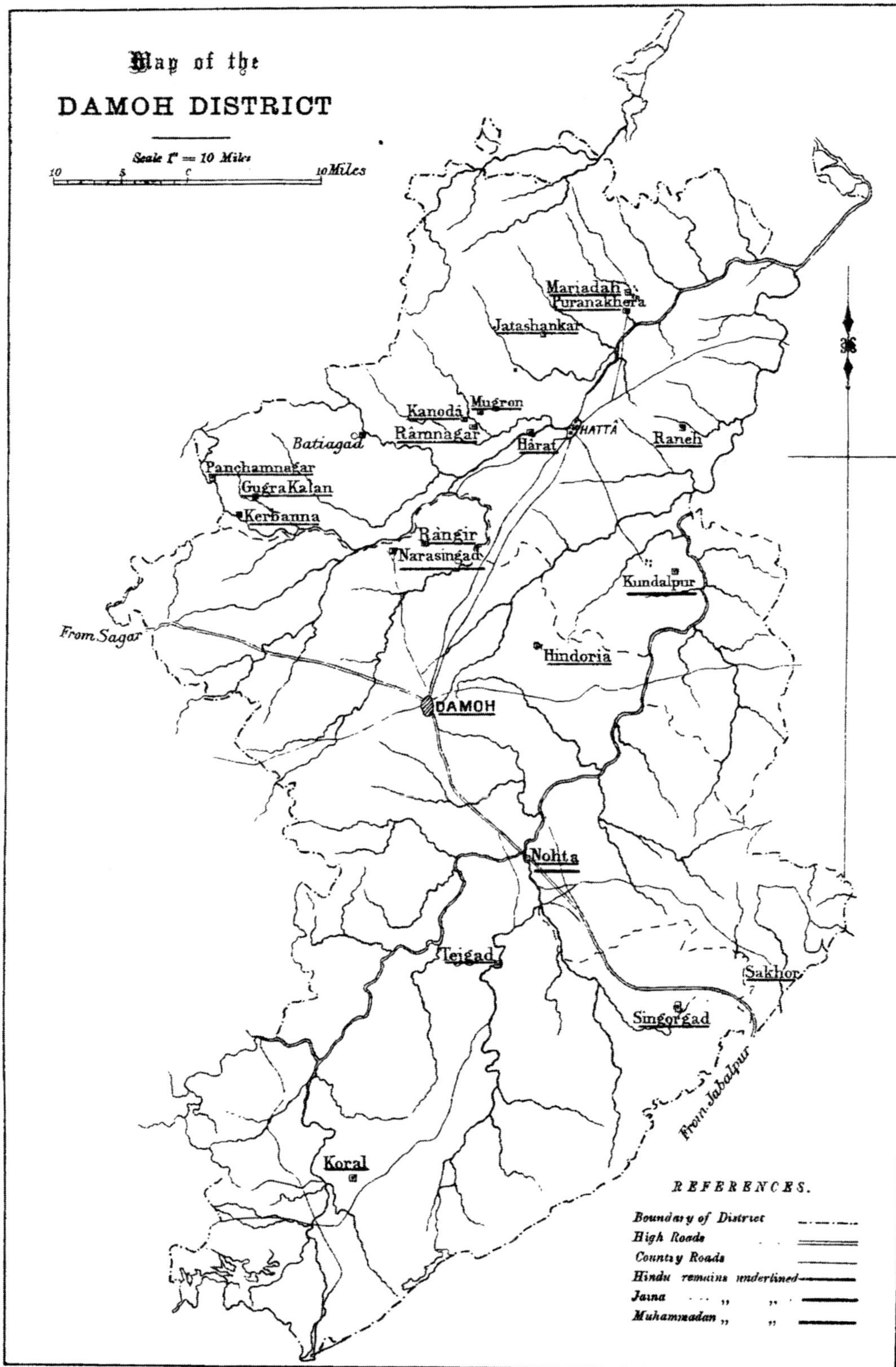

Reg No. 419 R. & A.—Mar 97.—410

Litho, S I O., Calcutta

of the Gond kings, and in an islet in the Wardhâ, in the same direction, there is an exceedingly curious rock-temple, which, during several months of the year, is fathoms under water. It is known as the Râma Tîrtha, and in A.D. 1866 was thoroughly cleaned out and explored.

Near the Râma Tîrtha, in the village of Sasti in the Nizam's dominions, there are three caves cut in the rock, in each of which there is said to be a *linga*.

In 1242 A.D., Khandkya Ballâlshâh X was reigning. He was living at Mowad; once he wished to pay a visit to Ballâlpur, where one of his predecessors had reigned. He therefore came to Ballâlpur and commenced to build the fort and the palace. He built the fort walls on the north-west and east sides. On the southern side he built a mud wall. In 1790 A.D., Vyankâji *alias* Nânâ Sâheb Bhonsle repaired the fort.

There was a small house which contained an idol of Keśavanâtha made of lead and plated with gold under a *nim* tree in front of the king's palace. Keśavanâtha was the family god of the Gond kings. In 1818 the idol was stolen away at the time of the war between the British and the Bhonsles. In 1822 one Pung Patel More, a *Kamâvisdâr*, placed a stone idol in the town instead of the old metal one stolen away.

Mr. Crawford, who was Superintendent, sanctioned a *nemnûk* for the temple. It is now converted into promissory notes which yield an annual interest of Rs. 24, which is taken by the family priest of the Gond kings, by name Andarkar.

There is also a temple of Kharji (or Khandkya Ballâlshâh) which was built in memory of Khandkya Ballâlshâh in 1282 A.D. Side by side with the tomb there is another tomb without any superstructure. It is said to be of Nîlkanthshâh, XIXth of the Gond kings. He died in 1751.

To the rear and front of the tomb of Khandkya Ballâlshâh there are two smaller ones said to be of his wives.

In front of the tomb of Khandkya Ballâlshâh there is a stone on which are carved 84 representations of feet in pairs, about which the local tradition is that when Khandkya died his 42 wives performed *sati* with him.

6. **Bhándak,** 16 miles north-west of Chândâ. The village of Bhâṇḍak would appear, from the numerous antiquarian remains, scattered in and around it, to have been a place of considerable note in olden times. Among the principal of these are:—

III. (1) The old fort, which is on the west side of the village and is partly ruined.

III. (2) The temple of Bhadrinâtha, a short distance to the south of the village, which is a structure recently rebuilt from the material of an older temple and partly with fresh materials. A small courtyard and *dharmaśâlâ* are attached to it, the latter having been built by Agriva Svâmi of Chândâ. Many old sculptures are built into the front wall of the temple, and lie loose about the courtyard, such as Gaṇapati, Vishṇu, Lakshmi-Nârâyaṇa, Śiva-Pârvati, Varâha, etc. The exterior of the temple is built and plastered in a plain simple manner with no attempt at architectural display. The object of worship is the Nâga. Lying beside the temple is an **inscription** slab.

III. (3) Immediately to the east of the last temple is a long high knoll, which seems to be artificial, upon which stand, apparently in position, all that remains of a former temple, *viz.*, two pairs of door-jambs which face west, quantities of dressed and carved blocks lying about, with a huge stone bowl and a figure of Gaṇapati.

II*b*. (4) About 500 yards west of the village, on the edge of a small old masonry tank, are the remains of a very old temple. It is very plain in design and is built of large square massive blocks. A number of old images are placed within. The building is partly ruined. Lying a few yards to the south of the temple, by the side of the pathway leading to the tank, is a life-sized representation of Śesha.

III. (5) In the field between the last and the village are the remains of another temple consisting merely of four pillars supporting cross-beams.

III. (6) On the south of the village, and adjoining it, is a cave in the rock which is now partly filled in with earth. It is unfinished and consists of a long verandah supported outwardly by two heavy, massive, octagonal pillars. Off the back wall are three unfinished cells. In the cell at the north end has been placed a ten-armed *devi*.

II*a*. (7) About a mile and a half to the south-west of the village, in the hill of Vinjhâsan, is a very curiously planned Buddhist cave. A long gallery is driven straight into the hill to a distance of 71 feet at the end of which is a shrine containing a colossal Buddha seated upon a bench. On the right and left of the entrance to this gallery other galleries, one on either side, are driven in at right angles to this first one, and each of these have a shrine and colossal Buddha. On the scarped side of the approach to the entrances to these galleries is a very much worn **inscription** in cave character. It is too faint to give an impression and can only be seen with the sun shining on the rock at an angle.

II*a*. (8) To the east of the village near the main road is a tank in which is an island. Connecting the island with the mainland is an old Hindu bridge constructed of massive columns in two rows with great heavy beams spanning the tops of these both transversely and longitudinally. Its total length is 136 feet and its width over all 7 feet 2 inches. On the mainland near the end of the bridge is a very extensive artificial mound, now overgrown with jungle, covered with carved blocks and sculptures, indicating the site of a large temple. On the island is the site of a small shrine.

II*b*. (9) In a small private enclosure on the south of the village are two colossal sculptures. The one represents Narasinha and measures 6 feet in height. The second is a representation of the *tâṇḍava*. Both figures have been well carved.

II*b*. **7. Bhatâla,** 10 miles north of Warorâ.

Bhatâla is supposed to have formed part of the ancient Bhadrâvati. On a long hill near the village are the remains of a very fine ancient temple, lofty and in good preservation, and the whole hill bears traces of having been fortified. The temple is in the custody of the *mâlguzâr*. Also the temple of Sri Hari Mahârâja which was built about 160 years ago by Devajipant Chorghade, the Divân of the great Râghoji.

It contains but little more than a score of houses, and derives its name from a beautiful group of temples which stand on a high bluff overlooking the river. The principal temple takes its name from Mârkaṇḍa Ṛishi, but it is dedicated to Śiva, whose *linga* is enshrined in the sanctum. The group comprises a monastery and is enclosed in a quadrangle, 196 feet by 118 feet, with entrances from the river front and the two sides, while along the rear side runs a row of cells facing the Wen Gangâ. The buildings themselves are of great antiquity, but much of the rich carving which adorns the temple appears to be of later date. General Sir A. Cunningham counted twenty-four temples.

(1) The temple of Màrkâṇda Ṛishi is by far the largest of the group, and is also the most elaborately sculptured. About 200 years ago it was struck by lightning, when the upper part of the massive spire was hurled down on to the roof of the *mahâ maṇḍapa*, which was broken in, and at the same time a small temple was utterly destroyed. The roof of the hall was repaired about 120 years ago, but in a very rude manner, by one of the Gond Ràjâs, whose architect introduced huge piers with radiating arches inside the principal room. The whole surface of the temple is covered with statues and ornament, there being upwards of four hundred figures alone.

(2) The pavilion of Nandikeśvara faces the Mârkaṇḍa temples on the east. It is a shrine for the bull Nandi, and is, in fact, part of the first temple.

(3) The second temple in size is named after Mârkaṇḍa Ṛishi, who is said to have been a son of Mṛikaṇḍu. It consists of a hall 27 feet 6 inches by 25 feet, two-thirds open, a small ante room and a sanctum. In the middle of the hall are four richly carved pillars supporting the roof. Over the shrine rises a lofty spire, which is nearly perfect, and is a very graceful specimen of its kind. The temple is dedicated to Śiva and has his *linga* in the shrine.

(4) A small temple 10 feet by 7 feet contains a symbol of Śiva]called "Jodh (?) Linga." It stands in front and to one corner of the last.

(5) Another temple dedicated to Śiva as Mṛityunjaya, or the "conquerer of death." The temple, which is 18 feet 6 inches long by 10 feet broad, contains the usual *linga* in the sanctum, with figures of Gaṇeśa and Vishṇu in the hall, and a small figure of Gaṇeśa over the entrance to the shrine.

(6) A temple facing the last and dedicated to "Yama-dharmarâja." On each side of the door of the shrine is a very richly carved group of Śiva and Pârvati. It is 16 feet long by 10 feet broad.

(7) The temple of Umâ Maheśvara.

(8), and (10) to (22) are all dedicated to Śiva and contain *lingas*.

(9) Râja-râjeśvara is a simple *linga* without any traces of a temple.

(23) The temple of the *Daśa Avatâra*, or ten incarnations of Vishṇu, is an open cloister 75 feet long by 7 feet wide inside, placed against the western wall of the enclosure. It is divided into 12 compartments by pilasters, two of the divisions being probably intended for statues of Vishṇu, and the remaining ten for the *avatâras*. In each division there is a pedestal, but several of them are now empty.

Besides the above temples there are several curious old square pillars, which are apparently much more ancient than any of the temples. Nearly all of them are sculptured, and some of them are inscribed. The chief figures are soldiers, armed with battle-axe, bow, and quiver full of arrows, in an attitude of attack.

III. 28. **Maroti** of Fadnavis, 4 miles north-west of Mul. Here there is a small old Hemâdpanti temple, which, though small in size, is interesting in its details. It contains a *linga*.

III. 29. **Mundipár,** in the *Zamindari* of Goevardha. A *kothi* built of stone without mortar. No local history or tradition is available.

30. **Nágri,** see Wâgnak.

II*b*. 31. **Neri,** a town situated on a tributary of the Andhâri, 5 miles east-south-east of Chimur. The antiquities are two old forts in ruins, and an old temple of no small size and beauty, the pillars and carving of which resemble those met with in the cave temples at Ajanta. Of more modern construction are some graceful Pânchâla tombs in which husband and wife sleep side by side. The old temple is being rapidly undermined by water from the tank, and will probably soon fall.

III. 32. **Panori,** two miles north-east of Deotek. Here are the ruins of a small temple of laterite, similar to the one at Deotek; here, also, are several slabs precisely similar to the inscribed slab at Deotek, similarly grooved with a channel, but broken across and not inscribed. Several statues of Vishṇu, Lakshmi, and Nandi, and several *lingas*, lie scattered about. There are no traditions or inscriptions; the ruins lie on a small mound about 15 feet in height and about 30 feet in diameter.

III. 33. **Palebaras,** 21 miles west by south of Rangi and 22 miles north of Mul. An old Hemâdpanti temple.

III. 34. **Panjurni,** 6 miles north-west of Warorâ, a peculiarly shaped temple said to have been built on the site of a *sati*, and in the centre of the building is seen a tomb with a figure representing a woman kneeling on the funeral pile previous to its being fired.

III. 35. **Rájgaḍ** is a large village on the road between Chândâ and Mârkaṇḍi. It possesses an old temple of Mahâdeva which, though small in size, is interesting for its details, as it is generally in very good preservation. The temple is dedicated to Mahâdeva whose *linga* is enshrined inside. The style is the same as that of the Mârkaṇḍi temples, and the roof of the sanctum is a pyramid rising in steps exactly like the pyramidal spires of the Daśa Avatâra temple at Mârkaṇḍa. (Cunningham's Reports, Vol. IX., p. 141.)

III 36. **Segáon,** a town 13 miles north-east of Warorâ. There is here an old stone fort in ruins with a handsome gateway.

III. 37. **Thánegáon,** 4 miles south of Amori. A small temple and a tank, the former being of about the same age as that at Ârmori. (Cunningham's Reports, Vol. VII., p. 126.)

III. 38. **Tipagaḍ,** an old fort perched among the hills and jungles, 28 miles east of Wairagaḍ. It is extremely difficult of access, and, when reached, has nothing of any interest beyond its old walls and remains of some small rooms. (Cunningham's Reports, Vol. VII., p. 130.)

III. 39. **Wágnáth,** 10 miles to the east of Warorâ. Panchâyatana of Sâmbaśiva temple, built in the Hemâdpanti style.

III. 40. **Wágnak,** 2 miles south of Nâgri railway station. A very old and peculiarly shaped temple, built of solid slabs without mortar. Between Wâgnak and Nâgri are found stones set up such as are elsewhere seen in circles.

III. 41. **Warhá,** 10 miles east by south of Chândâ. An old temple with a broad flight of steps leading down to the Wardhâ river.

III. 42. **Yedda,** in the *Zamindâri* of Rangi. An old temple of Mahâdeva built in the Hemâdpanti style, in a dilapidated state.

Upper Godâvari.

III. 1. **Albaka,** chief village of an estate of the same name, 40 miles to the north of Dumagudem. Some cromlechs, etc., on the hills, and close to the village.

III. 3. **Bhadráchallam,** about 140 miles from Sironcha. It owes its importance to an old and well-known temple of Râmachandra, which is situated on an eminence in the village, and is supposed to have been built about 400 years ago by one Ṛishi Pratishṭha, but has been added to at subsequent periods by various Râjâs. It consists of a main building covered by a fine dome, and flanked by smaller temples on both sides. The space in the centre is paved, and there is a stone *maṇḍapa*, or open flat-roofed building, in front of the chief shrine. The temples are surrounded by a high wall and from the river side are entered by a flight of steps. Religious observances are supported by a money grant of R13,000 (Haidarabad currency) per annum. The jewels belonging to the temple are said to be very valuable.

III. 4. **Parnasálá.** A temple connected with that at Bhadrâchallam.

III. 5. **Sironcha.** Some prehistoric stone sarcophagi, now in the Nâgpur Museum, are said to have been brought from here. More information needed.

IV.—Bhandârâ.

III. 1. **Bhandârâ.** At Bhandârâ itself are an old Hemâdpanti temple in the heart of the town containing two images called Ambâi and Nimbâi, which are daily worshipped; an old fort said to have been built by a Gavali king, now used as a jail; the Khâmb *talâv* also ascribed to a Gavali king having a pillar in the middle of it and two temples on its banks one of which is dedicated to Mahâdeva and one to Mâruti; a shrine with a little carving in places; and some tombs in charge of a *chelâ*, and having rent-free grounds attached for maintenance.

III. 2. **Adyar,** 17 miles south of Bhandârâ. A small temple, 12ft. by 10ft., of Mahâdeva ascribed to Hemâdpant, but said to be built of bricks, stone, and mortar. Also another small temple of similar workmanship, and a blackstone, well-carved, life-sized image of Pârśvanâtha which was discovered some nine years ago when excavating a foundation.

III. 3. **Ambagaḍ,** 18 miles north of Bhandârâ. This fort is said to have been principally used as a State prison for criminals of distinction, who were sent there to die of its bad climate and bad water; it is not of any interest otherwise: the gate of the fort faces east. (Cunningham's Reports, Vol. VII., p. 109.)

III. 4. **Amgáon,** the principal town of the chiefship of that name. In the neighbourhood, at a place called Padmapur, there are some curious old remains of massive stone buildings, but their origin is unknown.

III. 5. **Bijli,** a chiefship on the north-east border of the Bhandârâ district. Near the pass (Darekasâ) there are some curious caves in the adjoining hills, partly natural and partly artificial. They are called "Kachagaḍ" or the fort of safety. They have a good water-supply from a spring close by.

III. 6. **Brambi,** near Pipalgâon, 25 miles south of Bhandârâ, an old well constructed of great long stones, and ascribed to giants.

III. 7. **Chakaheti,** 40 miles north of Bhandârâ, a small Hemâdpanti temple measuring 10 feet by 8 feet on the road running from Chakaheti to Kusha.

III. 8. **Chandpur.** On the hills above the village of Chandpur the Gavalis erected a rough, but effective, fortified residence. The site of it is now marked only by a half broken wall.

III. 9. **Chichgaḍ,** about 2 miles from Darekasâ station on the Bengal-Nâgpur Railway. There is here a cave in which is a deity worshipped once or twice a year by the Gonds.

III. 10. **Gáimukh,** 20 miles north of Bhandârâ. A cave, in which is an image of Pârvati devi worshipped on *Śivarâtri.*

III. 11. **Ganeshtola** of Âmgâon. Âmgâon is a station on the Bengal-Nâgpur Railway. A very small Hemâdpanti shrine, but of no account.

III. 12. **Kámtha,** 24 miles east of Tirrora railway station. An old temple, 20 feet by 20 feet, but of no particular account.

III. • 13. **Korambi,** about 3 miles north-west of Pauni. On the side of the hill south of the village, distant a mile and a half or so, and facing the north, is to be found a cave temple with a figure of Mahâdeva in it. The people of the neighbourhood frequently resort to this place for worship. The road up the hill has been roughly made, and the hill is covered with bushy jungle. The cave is about 300 yards from the foot of the hill. The entrance is big enough only for a man to creep in. It consists of two compartments, the outer is about 6ft. by 4ft., while the inner, where the image is, is about the same. The outer room is too low for a person to stand erect, but the inner will allow of this. The image is about a foot high, and beside it there is no other sculpture.

III. • 14. **Korambi,** 3 miles south-west of Bhandârâ. An old temple constructed of large blocks of stone, with a low verandah in front. It measures 33ft. by 13ft., and is perched upon the summit of a hill upon the bank of the Wen Gangà. It is ascribed to Hemâdpant. In the front inner wall is an **inscription** in old character difficult to decipher.

III. 15. **Murmari,** 12 miles east of Bhandârâ. There is here the tomb of an English lady, the wife, as the **inscription** records, of Major Claye Watson, who died here in 1831 or 1851—the inscription is not very distinct. The tomb is now worshipped by the people of the neighbouring villages under the name of the "*kabar,*" the tomb, and "*deval,*" the shrine, and offerings are made. (Cunningham's Reports, Vol. XVII., p. 1.)

III. 16. **Nagra,** about 2 miles from Gundia station. A small old dilapidated temple about 12 feet by 10 feet.

17. **Padampur,** or Padmapur. See Amgâon.

III. 18. **Partápgaḍ fort,** about 40 miles south-east of Bhandârâ. The story goes that a man-eating demon had fixed his abode on the flat-topped eminence that we know as Partâpgaḍ. From this vantage-ground (the height of the hill and singularity of its shape make it a prominent feature in the landscape) he was accustomed to scan what passed in the country below; any ill-fated beings forced to pass that way were sure to be swallowed up by this monster. At last there came a saint who took up his abode at the foot of the hill on which the bluff rock of Partâpgaḍ stands. Soon the demon, aware of his presence, came to make a meal of him. A frightful battle ensued. At the end of the seventh day the demon was vanquished, and the victorious man of God erected a "house of victory" in commemoration of the event. This he made over to a Gond Râjâ, who took care in future to be himself the master of such an important position. It was always held as a Government post, and, like most of the others, was in the hands of the adherents of Appâ Sâheb. It was eventually reduced by Captain Gordon.

III. 19. **Pauni,** about 32 miles south of Bhandârâ. A fort, some Hindu temples of sorts, and several other miscellaneous buildings, but nothing of any age or interest.

III. 20. **Pinglâi,** a suburb of Bhandârâ town. A small Hemâdpanti temple containing the image of Pinglâi *devi*.

III. 21. **Pipalgáon,** 25 miles south of Bhandârâ. A plain stone pillar five feet long by one foot broad called the "Giant's Sarota."

III. 22. **Sanghari,** situated between the two famous lakes of Seoniband and Navegâon. It is a small fort which in 1818 was given up to the British. It is now a ruin.

III. 23. **Telota Khairi,** 24 miles south of Bhandârâ. A cromlech formed of one huge stone placed upon two other upright ones. There are also three stones set up on edge forming three sides of a square and called the Giant's Telota.

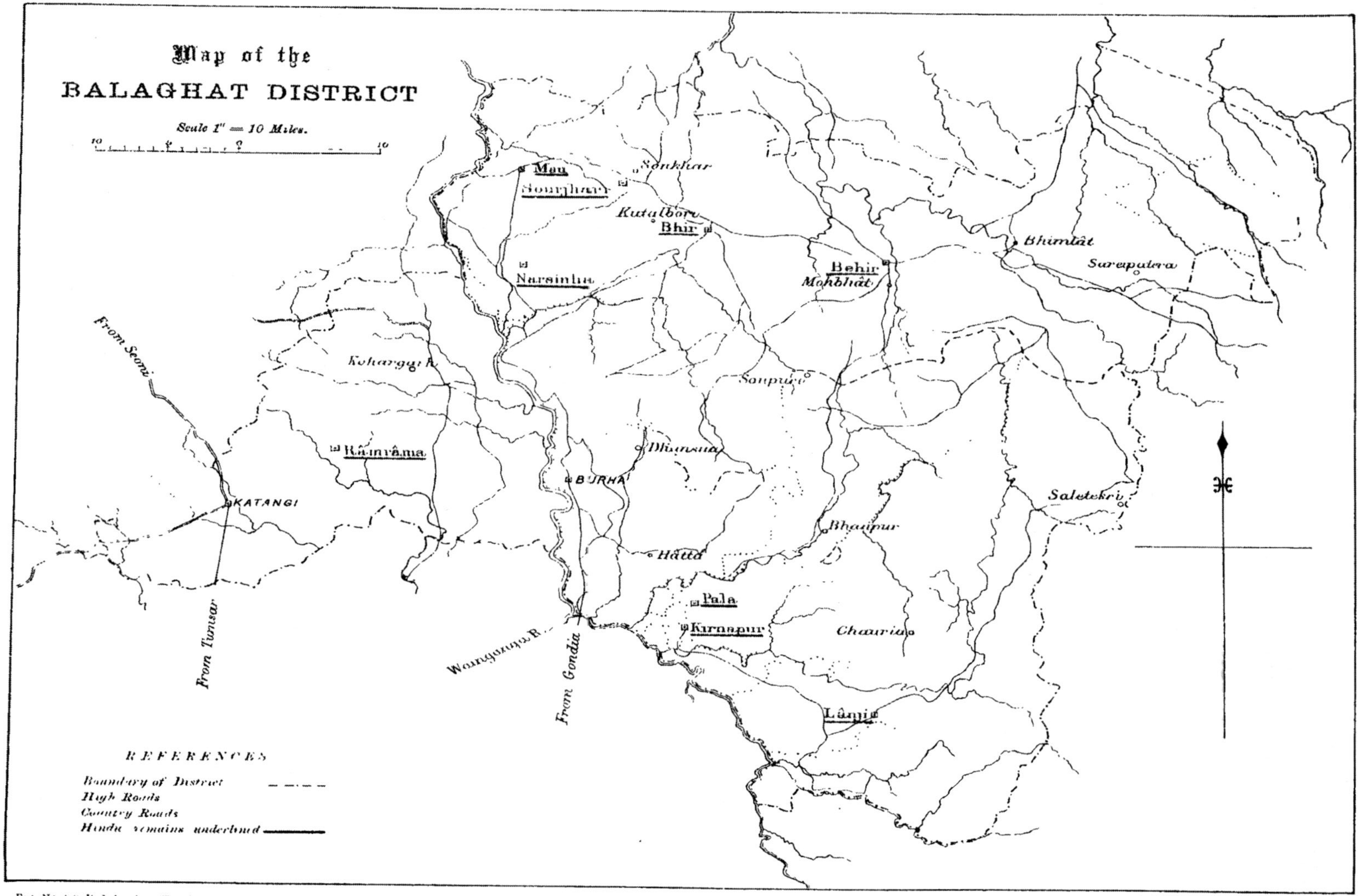

Reg. No. I.-G. R. & A.—Jan. 97.—410.

Litho. S. I. O. Calcutta.

V.—Bâlaghât.

III. 1. **Behir,** about 15 miles east of Parasvârâ. About a mile to the north of the town are some old temples, but of no particular merit.

III. 2. **Bhimlát,** 13 miles east of Behir and 28 miles east of Parasvârâ on the Banjar river. Near the village is a curious stone pillar or *lát*, lying on the ground in a grove of mango trees, which is said to be the *lát* of Bhîma. It is cut out of a peculiarly fine-grained stone, and seems to have been brought from a distance. There are, as is usual with these *láts*, several silly legends to account for it.

III. 3. **Bhir.** Here there are two plain and one carved Hemâdpanti temples, and one in ruins. There is a tank near them. They are all in a more or less dilapidated condition. There are no images in them. An image from one was sent in 1853 or 1854 by the Seoni district authorities to the Central Museum at Nâgpur. But there are a few fragments of images, from which it appears that they are of Jaina origin.

III. 4. **Háttá,** about 80 miles north-east of Bhandârâ, and 8 miles to the east of the Wengangâ. An old fort; close to the entrance to the fort is a fine *bávali*.

III. 5. **Kirnapur,** about 16 miles to the south-east of Burhâ. Some old temples which are found in various parts of the town.

III. 6. **Kohargas,** 18 miles north-west of Burhâ, in *parganá* Karola. An old court-house. This is the court-house of the famous personage Alâ Udal, built of black stones. There are the remains of a very large gate on the northern side and also the remains of a second gate.

On the hill is a triangular stone called the cot of Sonâ Râṇi, wife of Alâ Udal.

III. 7. **Kutalbori,** 4 miles south of Bhiri outpost. Near a *saj* tree, there is a stone 2½ feet by 2 feet on which are two images resembling soldiers.

III. 8. **Lánji,** about 90 miles north-east of Bhandârâ and 40 miles east of Burhâ. The fort is believed to be the work of the Gonds in the early part of the 18th century. It is surrounded by a moat, and was, no doubt, once a place of considerable strength, but is now out of repair. In the bamboo jungles, a mile to the north-east of the town, is an old temple dedicated to Mahâdeva, surrounded by what are said to be the remains of the original town.

III. 9. **Mau** outpost. One mile east is the Nâga *chabutrâ* in the midst of a tank 8 feet square and the same in height, of granite, on which is an image of a *nâga* and a pillar. There is also a temple with remains of a flight of steps. On the north of it are two images, one of Gaṇapati, the other a *piṇḍi* of Mahâdeva. The temple is said to have been built at the time of one Nowjadar, but who he was is not known. Two miles east of Mau outpost is a very old *nagârkhâna* built of stone, about 300 feet in height, said to have been constructed in the time of Alâ Udal when his marriage with Sonâ Râṇi of Kohargadh was celebrated, as a place for the blowing of horns, trumpets, and the sounding of other musical instruments.

There are traces of other old buildings here.

III. 10. **Mohbhat,** one and a half miles south of Behir. A "*madhi*" supported on four monolith pillars. Near it is a granite image.

III. 11. **Narsinha,** 4 miles north of Charegâon outpost in Mau *tâluka*. Temple of Narasinha, a small but very old temple. It stands on a semi-spherical granite hill of the name of Narasinha.

III. 12. **Pála,** 2 miles north-west of Kirnapûr. A temple called "Brahmachâri," partly plain and partly sculptured, 8 feet long by 5 feet broad by 19 feet high.

III. 13. **Rámráma,** 18 miles west of Burhâ. A "*sthâna*" of Mahâdeva, 150′×200′, very old and built of plain black stone.

III. 14. **Sonkhar,** 8 miles east of Mau, on the hill of Sondardehi. Sadâ Bhadâ images.

In the remains of a very old fortress there are 53 images of stone called Sadâ Bhadâ images; one of them is the image of a rider with an umbrella over his head and a palanquin before him in which is the figure of a female. The third image is standing with a sword and shield in its hand. It is of a yellow colour and is called "Bhandia Sadâ." The rest are not of importance. The Gonds say that when Gonds were the rulers and when Sada Bhada was their king, and his marriage procession was going on, all the people in the procession with Sadâ Bhadâ were transformed into these images of stone.

III. 15. **Sourjhari,** 6 miles north-west of Bhiri. A natural cave containing an image of Mahâdeva. There are also images of Gaṇapati, Vishṇu, and Pârvati. All these images have been introduced within the last 30 years. The tradition is that this Mahâdeva goes to meet Narasinha *deva* on the Narsinha hill.

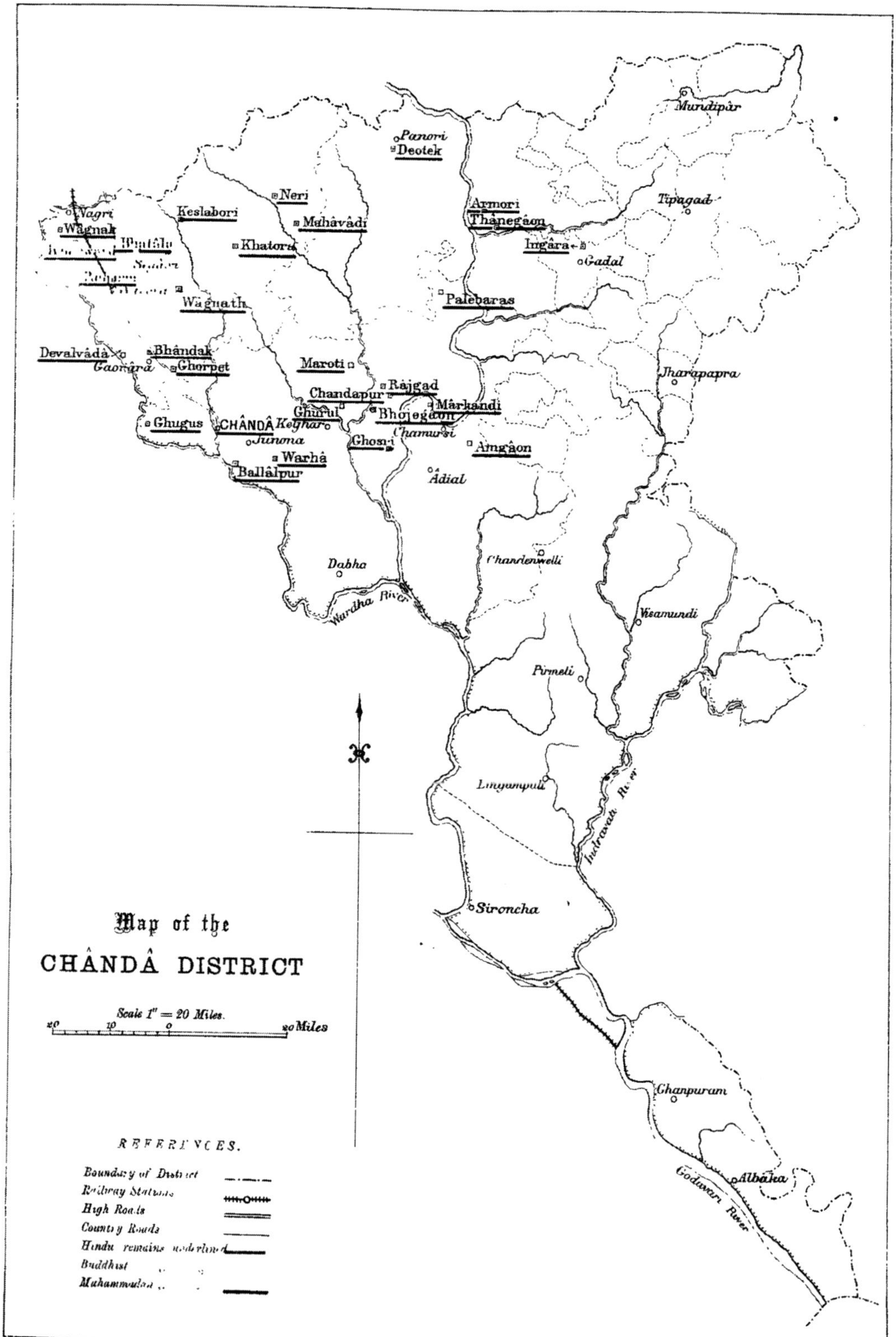

Map of the
CHÂNDÂ DISTRICT

Reg No 419 R & A —Mar 97 —420

Litho., S. I. O. Calcutta

III. 8. **Bhojegáon,** 5 miles south of Mul, temple of Mahâdeva, said to be built in the Hemâdpanti style.

III. 9. **Chámursi,** 39 miles east of Chândâ, a group of 20 cromlechs or kistvaens.

III. 10. **Chandapur,** 5 miles south-east of Mul, a temple of Mahâdeva in the Hemâdpanti style.

III. 11. **Churul,** 6 miles to the south-west of Mul, the temple of Keśavanâtha built in the Hemâdpanti style.

III. 12. **Deotek,** 4 miles north-east of Nagbir and 22 miles south-west of Pauni; a small temple with the remains of a second, also an **inscription.** (Cunningham's Reports, Vol. VII., p. 125.)

III. 13. **Devalvádá.** The hill of Devalvâdâ is situated six miles and a half to the west of Bhânḍak. On the top is a small square fort, now in ruins, with four pillars of an old temple standing within. There is also a dry tank. In the side of the hill are several caves, of which the largest is called "Narasinha." (Cunningham's Reports, Vol. IX., p. 135.)

III. 14. **Gaorára,** or Gavarâra, is a small village situated one mile and a half to the south of Bhânḍak. To the west are several fine tanks, beyond which is a low hill crowned with the remains of several temples. There are also many detached rocks, several of which have been hollowed out to form caves and niches. The principal temple is called Jobnasa's palace, and the two chief caves are called his big and little fowl-houses. (Cunningham's Reports, Vol. IX., p. 133.)

III. 15. **Ghorpet.** At the village of Ghorpet, between Bhânḍak and Chândâ, there was once a fine temple which has been utterly destroyed by a gigantic *pipal* tree the roots of which now hold together a portion of its walls with one pilaster and several mouldings complete. This *pipal* tree is 9 feet in diameter, and 29 feet in circumference. The pilaster is remarkable for being built up in regular courses of stone with the walls instead of being a monolith. The remains were formerly much more extensive, but the stones are said to have been carried away by a road officer to build a bridge. The pilaster is a very fine example of the style of mouldings of the mediæval temples of this part of the country. (Cunningham's Reports, Vol. IX., p. 136.)

III. 16. **Ghosri,** 12 miles south of Mul, a temple of Mahâdeva in the Hemâdpanti style, in a dilapidated state.

III. 17. **Ghugus,** 13 miles west of Chândâ, three cave-temples. These are in the rocky ground near Ghugus. There is an idol of "Bhairanadeva" in one of them. The legs of the idol are broken off. The local tradition regarding this is that in former times several thefts and dacoities used to take place, but none could be committed at

Ghugus. Consequently the thieves and dacoits cut off the legs of the idol. In front of the idol at a distance of about 5 or 6 cubits there is a stone standing erect. It is called Bàhi (sleeve of Sìtâ). Not far off there is another small cave which contains a stone, which the people say is the mother of Bhairanadeva. Between these two caves are two stones where a fight between a tiger and a wild boar is said to have taken place. The idol of Bhairanadeva was said to have been increasing in height. His mother therefore put a stone on the idol's head.

III. 18. **Ingára,** in the Rangi chiefship, and about 4 miles north of Rangi. Here there is an ancient temple, on which there is a carving of a warrior with a short straight sword and a shield.

III. 19. **Jhádá,** Pàpdâ, a cave in a hill.

II. 20. **Junona,** a village in the Chândâ district, situated 7 miles east of Chândâ. It possesses a very fine tank, on the stone embankment of which stand the remains of an ancient palace, and in its rear are traces of a wall 4 miles in length. In communication with the tank is an elaborate system of under-channels, some of which have evidently been injured, as a large volume of water now escapes by them.

III. 21. **Keljhar,** a large village about half way between Chândâ and Mârkaṇḍa. Two small cromlechs, said to be temples raised by the Kurumbâr shepherds.

III. 22. **Keslabori,** a village situated under the western slopes of the Chimur Hills, and 10 miles north-north-east of Segâon. In the vicinity, at the foot of a precipice, is the Râmdighi pool, hollowed out of the rock, about 40 feet in diameter, and of unknown depth; and into this basin falls, during the rains, a considerable stream from the precipice above. Tradition attributes the formation of the pool to Râma: and on an eminence above is an ancient temple, in which are two good carvings of a warrior with shield and straight sword. The temple is falling to ruins.

III. 23. **Kharward,** 8 miles to the east of Warorâ. A ruined temple in the Hemâdpanti style.

III. 24. **Khatora,** a village about 26 miles north of Chândâ. There are the remains of a considerable stone fort with a moat and double lines of defences. Near one of the bastions is the tomb of Chând Khân, who is much venerated by the Musalmans of the district.

III. 25. **Mahávádi,** 46 miles north-east of Warorâ. Has a dilapidated temple in the Hemâdpanti style.

III. 26. **Márana,** in the *Zamindari* of Rangi, is said to have a cave, concerning which there is neither history nor tradition.

I*b*. 27. **Márkandi,** a village situated on the left bank of the Wen or Venya Gangâ river, 3 miles north-north-west of Châmursi and about 40 east of Chândâ.

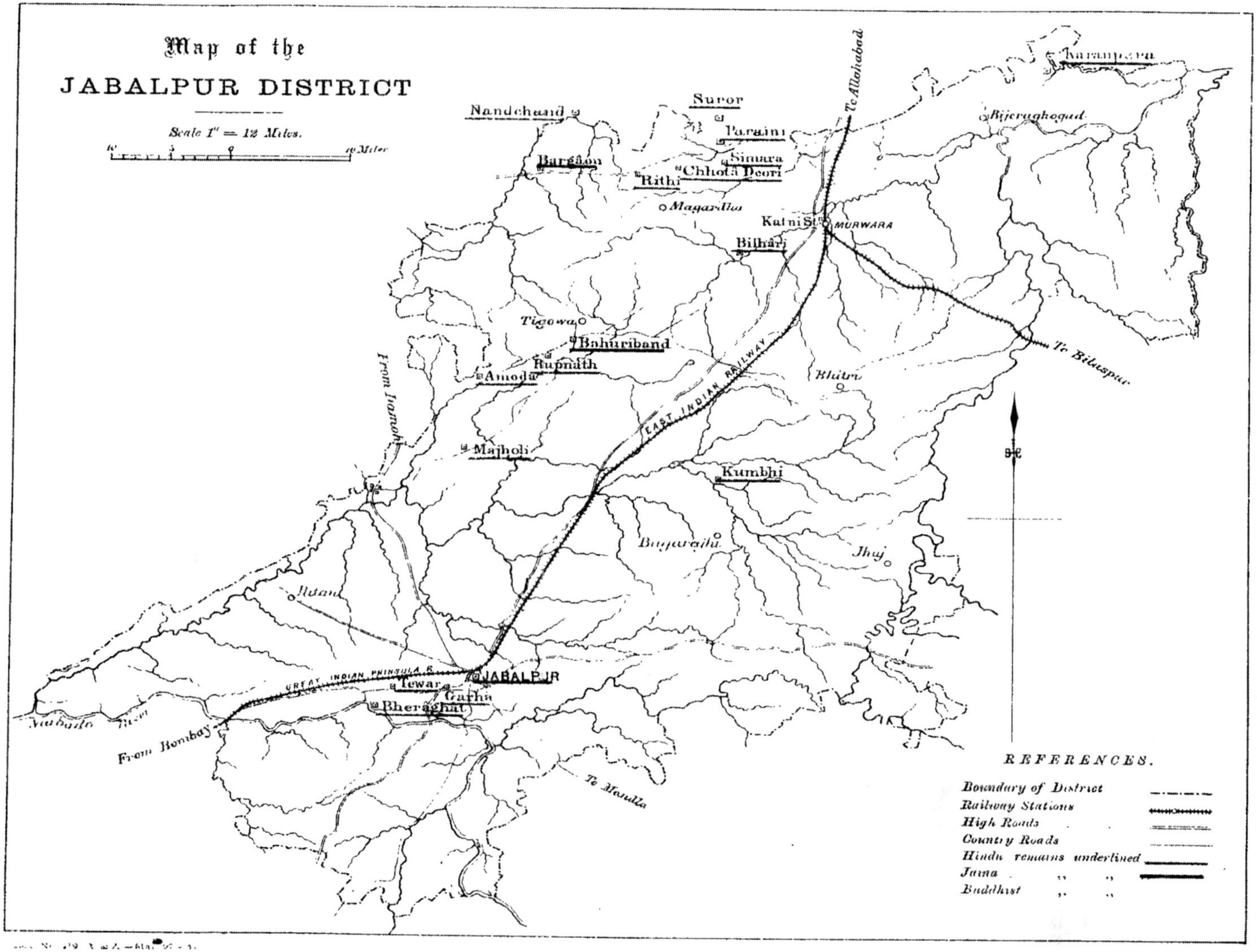

Litho., S. I. O., Calcutta.

II.—JABALPUR DIVISION.

I.—JABALPUR DISTRICT.

III. 1. **Jabalpur.** The only remains at Jabalpur itself are some Jaina statues collected and built into a masonry block in the garden of Messrs. Cursetjee and Co. They are well carved images.

III. 2. **Amoda.** The village of Amoda is situated on the crest of the Kaimur range 7 miles to the south-west of Bahuriband, and about 20 miles nearly due west from Sleemanâbâd. Amongst the *sati* monuments in the neighbourhood, there is one with an **inscription** dated in *Samvat* 1651, or A.D. 1594, during the reign of the Gond Râjà Prem Nârâyaṇa.

IIb. 3. **Bahuriband,** 12 miles west of Sleemanâbâd railway station, contains a colossal Jaina statue 12 feet 2 inches high, standing under a *banyan* tree near the town. On the pedestal is an **inscription** of seven lines. (Cunningham's Report, Vol. IX., p. 39.)

III. 4. **Balakoti,** about 9 miles to the south-west of Murwârâ and 15 miles due north of Sleemanâbâd. A fort which was constructed by the Lodis. It was partially destroyed after the mutiny of 1857-58. It is a comparatively modern building.

III. 5. **Bargáon,** half way between Damoh and Jokahi railway station. An old site of the Jains as shewn by remains of their temples and sculptures. One temple stands to a height of 21 feet above its basement. It contains a weather-worn and illegible **inscription.** (General Cunningham's Report, XXI., pp. 101 and 163.)

Ib. 6. **Bherághát,** 12 miles west of Jabalpur. This is a famous bathing-place on the Narmadâ. The river here runs calm and deep between the well-known "Marble Rocks." There are a few small temples close by of no particular merit, but upon the top of a conical hill just above the village are some remains of great interest. Here there is a temple surrounded by a circular colonnade or corridor. The temple is more or less modern, occupying the place of an older one which has disappeared. But the circular corridor which surrounds it is a far more ancient structure. It consists of a high circular wall against the inside of which is built a verandah, being supported along its inner side by columns set at regular intervals. The pilasters built against the wall opposite each of these pillars divide the wall space into panels or bays, and set against the wall, one in each of these, upon its own pedestal, are life-sized images of gods, goddesses, and others. The most of these still remain, but in a terribly mutilated condition. (For full account see General Cunningham's Report, IX., p. 60.)

III. 7. **Bhitri.** There are the remains of a fort on the hills near Bhitri.

III. 8. **Bijeraghogaḍ,** has a handsome but comparatively recent fort.

III. 9. **Bilhári,** 10 miles west of Katni railway station. Once a place of some note, but now only a wreck of its former self. The only remains of any consequence now existing at Bilhâri are the great tank of Lakshman Sâgara, the small tank of Dhabora Tâl, the Vishṇu-Varâha temple, and the ruined temple known as the palace of Kâma-Kandalâ. These remains are of great age. Sculptured stones and pillars from these have been greatly used in building the houses in the town.

II*b*. 10. **Chhotá Deori,** 16 miles west of Jokahi railway station. Near the sources of the Kiyân or Ken river are some small ruined temples. The best known of these is at Chhotâ Deori, where there is a famous pillar with an old **inscription** in characters of the 6th or 7th century.

III. 11. **Garhá,** four miles west of Jabalpur. This place was once the capital of the Gond dynasty of Garhâ Mandlâ, whose ancient keep, known as the Madana Mahâl, still crowns the low granite range, along the foot of which the town is built. Tradition gives Garhâ a great antiquity, and it probably existed before the Christian era. Its decline in importance dates from the time of the removal of the Gond dynasty to Singorgaḍ and subsequently to Mandlâ. The *mahâl* was built about A.D. 1100 by Madan Singh and is now a ruin. Under it to the west, is the beautiful Gangâ Sâgara tank, and near it is the large sheet of water called the Bâl Sâgara. The *mahâl* was a very plain small building of no architectural proportions, and its only interest lies in its picturesque position, perched as it is upon the very top of the hill upon a huge boulder of rock. It is a conspicuous object for miles around.

II*b*. 12. **Karanpara,** near Karitalai, 27 miles north-east of Murwârâ. A stone figure of the boar of Vishṇu, of enormous size and beautifully carved in red sandstone, called "Barah-rûp" (varâha). The village of Karitalai stands on the east side of the Kaimur range of hills 22 miles south of Maihar. The old name of the place was Karupur, which is now restricted to a small village, with a number of ruined temples lying along the ridge to the north of the modern town. There is also a large tank called "Sâgara," half a mile in length, to the east of the ruins, but is dry now. The temple containing the figure is in ruins. The carved stones, etc., might be collected and cared for.

III. 13. **Kumbhi.** The chief village of the *parganá* of the same name in the Jabalpur district, about 10 miles east by south of Sihora and 12 miles south of Sleemanâbâd. It is situated on rising ground on the banks of the Hiran and contains several temples.

III. 14. **Magardha.** An ancient village about 5 miles north of Bilhâri in Sleemanâbâd *tehsil*. A Gond fort in ruins.

IIb. 15. **Majholi.** The village of Majholi lies on the old road leading from Tewar (Tripura), the old capital of Chedi, to Bilhâri, being 22 miles to the north of the former, and 30 miles to the south-west of the latter. It once possessed a famous temple of Vishṇu, of which nothing now remains but a large statue of the *varâha* or boar incarnation of Vishṇu. The statue is almost hidden in the deep darkness of a modern temple, which has been built out of the ruins of the old fane, with numerous pieces of sculpture inserted in the wall. Close by is one of the ceiling slabs of the old temple, with its deeply cut squares and circles of ornamental moulding. This has been turned into a *chakki*, or mill-stone, for grinding lime. Nothing is known about the history of the temple—not even its name. Amongst the broken sculptures in the neighbourhood is a Hara-Gauri, or Śiva and his wife, seated, with a standing figure of Śiva and a squatted Jaina statue, naked as usual.

III. 16. **Nandchand.** A small village on an island at the junction of the Kundo *nâlâ* with the Patnâ river. On the bank of the Patnâ river are some fine Hindu remains, consisting of a ruined temple and a *torana* gateway with numerous statues. The place is forty miles east-north-east of Damoh. (See Cunningham's Report, XXI., p. 160.)

III. 17. **Paraini,** an old village on the right bank of the Ken river, 11 miles to the west of the Jokahi railway station. There are the ruins of several temples on the bank of a tank to the north of the village. The principal object is the statue of a boar 5 feet 3 inches long. (Cunningham's Report, XXI., p. 158.)

III. 18. **Rithi,** 18 miles to the north-west of Murwârâ. To the east of the village is a long heap of cut and carved stones, the remains of some ten or twelve temples. Numerous fragments of sculptures lying about. (Cunningham's Report, XXI., p. 160.)

19. **Rupnâth,** 14 miles due west of Sleemanâbâd and 3 miles south-west of Bahuriband. Rûpnâtha is the name of a famous *linga* of Śiva, which is placed in the cleft of a rock, where the Bunder Chûa *nâlâ* pours over the face of the Kaimur range of hills. The descent is made in three falls, each of which has a famous pool, which is also an object of worship. The uppermost is called the Râma Kuṇḍa, the middle one the Lakshmaṇa Kuṇḍa, and the lowest one the Sitâ Kuṇḍa. But the site of
Ib. Rûpnâtha is more interesting from the presence there of one of the rock inscriptions of Aśoka. (Cunningham's Report, Vol. IX., p. 38.)

III. 20. **Simara,** on the right bank of the Ken river, near the northern end of the Sati Pahâr, about 10 miles from Murwârâ and Katni stations. To the east of the village there are the ruins of four temples, one large and three small. On the embankment of the Badâ Tàl there are the ruins of a fifth temple. There is also a large slab with an inscription dated *Sam.* 1355. (Cunningham's Report, XXI., p. 159.)

III. 21. **Suror,** two and a half miles from Paraini, and 11 miles west of the Jukahi railway station. An old *sati* pillar with a curious **inscription** in five lines, dated *Sam.* 1328.

III. 22. **Tewar,** about 7 miles west of Jabalpur. About half a mile south-east of Tewar are the ruins of the old city of Tripura, now known as Karaṇbel. Tradition speaks loudly of the immense ruins of Karaṇbel, but the railway, with its insatiable capacity of absorbing to itself all workable stone within its influence, has long since so reduced the ruins that no remains are now left of any interest.

II*b*. At the west end of the village of Tewar, under a large tree, are collected together a great number of sculptures all more or less broken, but many of them otherwise in very good preservation, and most exceptionally well carved. Every one of them is said to have been brought from the site of the old city of Karaṇbel. The most perfect specimen is a Buddhist sculpture of "Vajrapâṇi," who is represented seated under a canopy with his hands in the teaching attitude assumed so often by Buddha in his images. Under the image is an **inscription.** For further description see General Cunningham's Reports, Vol. IX., p. 54.

II*a*. 23. **Tigowa,** 2 miles to the north of Bahuriband, and 13 west of Sleemanâbâd. Here there is a low rectangular mound, about 250 feet long by 120 feet broad, which is entirely covered with large blocks of cut stone. The ruins of many temples. Only one temple is now standing, that of Kankâli Devi. Originally it was a small single room, with an open portico in front, supported on four pillars, of the same type as those at Udayagiri and Eran. At this temple are two **inscriptions** on one of the pillars. About 60 feet to the north-east there is part of an entrance door of a second temple of a much larger size. But besides these two shrines can be traced the foundations of no less than thirty-six other temples, the largest of which being only 15 feet. The whole of these had been utterly destroyed by a railway contractor. (General Cunningham's Reports, Vol. IX., p. 41.)

II.—Damoh.

IIa. 1. **Damoh.** The head-quarters of the district of the same name. Most of the Hindu temples here were destroyed by the Muhammadans, and their materials were used to construct a fort, which, in its turn, has been destroyed, so that practically no buildings of interest remain. On the bank of the Phuteriâ tank are one or two modern temples, but upon the platform surrounding the base of a large tree between them, are gathered together a collection of more or less mutilated sculptures from some old temple. In the garden of the Deputy Commissioner's house are some more with a well-sculptured doorway, and a much abraided inscription slab under a tree near the well. In the Tehsildar's *kacheri* are two inscription slabs—one Sanscrit, the other Persian.

III. 2. **Batiagad.** An old town and fort about 20 miles north-west of Damoh.

III. 3. **Gugra Kalan,** 24 miles north-west of Damoh. A fort built by Râv Makhan Singh in the time of the Bundelas.

III. 4. **Hárat,** 3 miles south-west of Hattâ. A place of some importance under the Bundelas, but now only noticeable for some Muhammadan tombs.

III. 5. **Hattá,** 24 miles north-east of Damoh. The fort is said to have been built by the Gonds upwards of 500 years ago. It is built of rubble stone in lime. The Rang Mahâl, a kind of palace in the Marâthâ style inside the fort, was built in 1804 by Govind Râv of Sâgar, who strengthened the fort also.

The temple of Chând Devi is an old temple, dedicated to the goddess Devi. There is nothing remarkable about the architecture. The temple is esteemed especially sacred by the people of Hattâ, and is visited by all Hindu strangers also. It is said to have been built in the time of the Gond Râjâs; date unknown. It is especially resorted to during epidemics.

III. 6. **Hindcriá.** 10 miles north-east of Damoh. Here are numerous *sati* pillars, of which the oldest is dated *Samvat* 1113. There are also many carved stones and remains of temples. (Cunningham's Reports, XXI., p. 167.)

III. 7. **Jatashankar,** 7 miles north by west from Hattâ. A fort said to have been built by Fateh Singh, Amil of Fatehpur *pargana*, in *Samvat* 1700, in the time of the Bundelas. It is in fair preservation, but has long been left uninhabited. It is in the Marâthâ style and has some remarkably deep wells in it.

III. 8. **Kanodá,** 14 miles north-west of Hattâ. Has the remains of an old sculptured temple. In the time of the Bundela Râjâs, Amir Singh, Amil of Kanodâ, constructed the fort. It is a kind of summer sporting residence rather than a fort. It is in ruins and not worth preserving.

III. 9. **Kerbanna.** A fort 25 miles north-west from Damoh. Built by Râv Madhari Lodhi during the reign of the Chandeli kings. Most of it is in ruins, but some of the inside buildings are still inhabited by a Lodhi family. It is in the Marâthâ style.

III. 10. **Koral.** A temple, but of no particular interest.

III. 11. **Kundalpur,** 20 miles east of Damoh. Here there are some fifty more or less modern Jaina temples. At the foot of the hill, near the Vardhamâna *talâv*, are two old Brahmanical temples, both facing north. One is empty, but the other still holds a standing figure of Vishṇu. (General Cunningham's Reports, Vol. XXI., p. 166.)

III. 12. **Mariadah,** 10 miles north of Hattâ. A fort. It is now almost in ruins. It was built under Jugrâj Divân of Chattarsal of Punna. It is mixed in style. The bastions are of the older style, similar to Singorgaḍ, the inner building being in the Marâthâ style.

III. 13. **Mugron,** 7 miles west of Hâttâ. The ruins of an old temple said to have been built in the time of the Gond Râjâs, but it is now of no particular interest.

III. 14. **Narasingaḍ,** 12 miles north-west of Damoh, on the right bank of the river Sunâr. During the period of Muhammadan ascendancy it was known as "Nasratgarh," but this was changed into the present name by the Marâthâs. A fort and a mosque are the only relics of the Muhammadans. A second fort erected by the Marâthâs, was partially destroyed by the British troops in 1857. Most of the better buildings are now in ruins.

Ia. 15. **Nohtá,** 13 miles south-east of Damoh. Judging from the number of sites of old temples, which are scattered in and around the village, Nohta must have been at one time a place of note. The only old temple now standing is near the road, about half a mile to the south of the village. It is in a very ruinous condition, the outer shell of the walls of the shrine having for the most part fallen together with the *śikhara* and roof of the *sabhâ maṇḍapa*. The temple consists of a shrine, hall, and porch, which have all been fully decorated. Beside Hindu shrines, there would appear to have been one or more Jaina temples, since Jaina figures are also found lying about the place, amongst them being a figure of Chandraprabha. Pillars, lintels, sculptures, and other fragments are found throughout the village built into the walls of houses and enclosures.

16. **Panchamnagar,** 24 miles north-west of Damoh. Fort, built by Râjâ Hirde Shâh in the reign of the Bundela Râjâs. Now in ruins.

III. 17. **Puranakera,** 9 miles north of Hattâ. Fort. One Nanzoo Lodhi is said to have constructed the fort during the time of Râjâ Chattarsal of Punna. It is in ruins. There is nothing remarkable about the architecture.

III. 18. **Râmnagar,** 9 miles west by north of Hattâ. A fort, built in *Samvat* 1823 by Gandharap Singh Lodhi, whose heirs are in possession and keep it in repairs.

III. 19. **Raneh,** 8 miles to the east of Hattâ. A temple, said to have been built by Rechariya Brahmâns 500 years ago in the time of the Chandeli kings. It has an **inscription** which is illegible. There are several families of Rechariyas still living in the village.

III. 20. **Rángir,** 12 miles north of Damoh. A fort. About 190 years ago (Pausha *Vadya* 3, *Samvat* 1760). This fort was constructed by Rachori during the time of Chattarsal of Punna, for sporting purposes. It is almost in ruins. It is in the same style as Jatâshankar fort (No. 7).

III. 21. **Sakhor.** A temple, said to have been built during the reign of the Chandeli kings, with an illegible **inscription.**

II*a*. 22. **Singorgaḍ.** A hill fort situated 28 miles south-east of Damoh.

The fort is a Gond one, built in rubble stone masonry and is now in ruins. The people attribute it to one Râjâ Bel, a prince of the Chandela Rajput tribe (Central Provinces' Gazetteer, p. 480). But General Cunningham (*vide* his Report on a tour in the Central Provinces, vol. ix, pages 48 to 54) attributes it to one Gaj Singh, a Parbar Râjput, and considers it was built in *Samvat* 1360, answering to A.D. 1307; and that it was enlarged by Dulpat Shâh of Garba Mandla, who moved the seat of government there (*vide* page 50).

The widow of Dulpat Shâh, the famous Râṇi Durgâvati, was defeated near here by Asaf Khân, an officer of the great Akbar; and the fort is said to have stood a siege of nine months in the days of Aurangzib. It must have been of immense size. The remains of the outer circumvallation are still most extensive. Of the citadel or inner fort, which is on a high central hill, little remains but a solitary tower and some ruined water reservoirs. Two smaller towers still stand on neighbouring hills.

III. 23. **Tejgaḍ,** 20 miles south of Damoh. A fort. It is comparatively modern and is built of rubble stone set in mud. Built by the Lodhis.

III.—Sâgar.

III. 1. **Ságar.** The principal town in the district of the same name, which is said to be the Sageda of Ptolemy. There is a fort here which was commenced by the Râjputs in A.D. 1660, but was completed as it now stands by the Marâthâs about one hundred years ago. It stands on the north-west bank of the lake at a considerable elevation commanding the whole of the city and surrounding country. It has been built on no particular plan, but so as to take the best advantage of the ground on which it stands. It consists of twenty round towers, varying from 20 to 40 feet in height, connected by thick curtain walls, and enclosing a space of six acres. This space is for the most part covered with old Marâthâ buildings of two storeys. Since the accession of the British Government, a magazine, a large building now used for medical stores, and a barrack, beside other small buildings for the magazine stores, etc., have been constructed. There is only one place of exit and entrance on the east side.

II*b*. In the garden of the artillery mess-house (1894)—one in each of the four corners—are collections of old sculptures built up into small imitation kiosks. On the west face of that in the south-west corner is a partly abraided **inscription.** A few more sculptures lie in the garden of the house used by the office of the District Council.

III. 2. **Binaika,** about 24 miles north of Sâgar. A fort.

III. 3. **Dhamoni,** 29 miles north of Sâgar. A fort, which is almost in ruins, stands on an eminence at a short distance from the summit of the *ghâts* leading to Bunḍelkhanḍ and commands the valley of the river Dhasan. It is of a triangular ground plan and encloses a space of 52 acres. The ramparts are in general fifty feet high and in most parts 15 feet thick, with enormous round towers. There are besides interior works strengthening the defences of the eastern quarter, where the magazine and officers' quarters were probably situated.

I*a*. 4. **Eran,** on the south bank of the Bina river, 6 miles north-east of Bâmorâ station on the I. M. Railway. There is here a most interesting collection of remains upon high ground above the bank of the river, and about half a mile west of the village. There were here at one time more than half a dozen small Vaishṇava temples, but now nothing remains of the temples themselves save some of the lower courses of masonry, four standing columns with their architraves, a colossal Varâha, a gigantic image of Vishṇu, a broken one of Narasinha, with many beams, sculptures, and parts of doorways lying about. But more interesting than all this is a great stone column 47 feet high, which stands out before the temples, and contains an old Gupta **inscription.** Beside it stands another smaller column but without an inscription. There is a second **inscription** upon the throat of the colossal Varâha. In the village

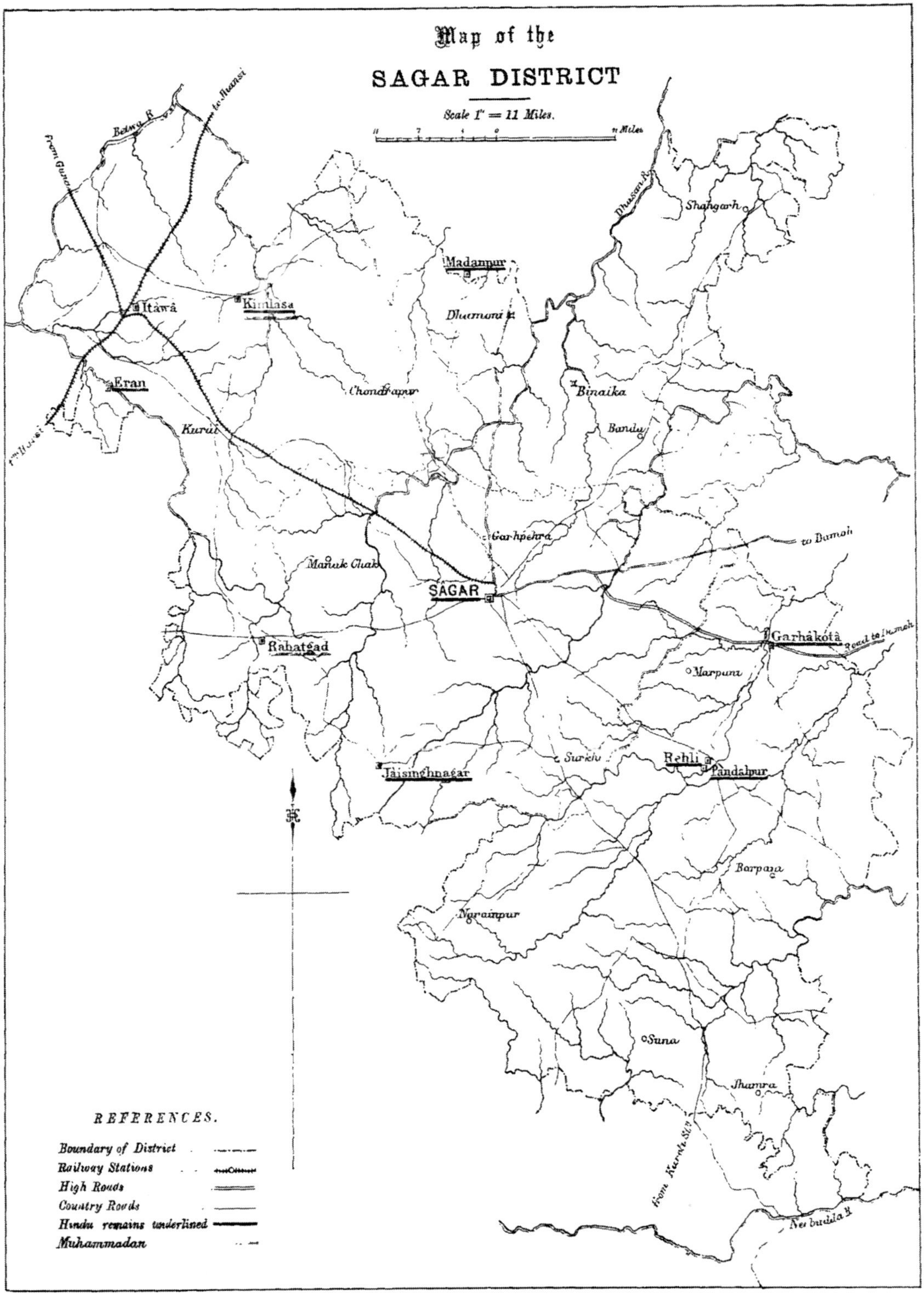

Reg No 419, R & A—Feb 97—410

Litho. S. I. O., Calcutta

within the courtyard of a house, is a large image of Varâha with one line of **inscription** in very old characters. An old **inscription** on an octagonal *linga* at the hamlet of Pelichpur about 2 miles from Eran. For fuller account of Eran and its remains see General Cunningham's Report, VII., p. 88.

III. 5. **Garhákotá,** 28 miles east of Sâgar. A fort, mostly in ruins, situated on a lofty eminence to the east of the town, between the rivers Sunâr and Gadhairi. A natural moat is thus formed on three sides of it, and on the fourth side an artificial one has been constructed. The place, both from its natural advantages, and the solidity and excellence of its construction, must have been one of enormous strength, and, without large guns, almost impregnable. The inner walls enclose a space of eleven acres, the greater part of which is covered with buildings and palaces. These are, for the most part, now in ruins, as are also the outer walls and bastions. The latter were breached by Sir Hugh Rose in 1858, when the fort was taken, and were afterwards partly levelled by sappers.

About two miles north of the town, on the borders of a large forest (the Ramnâ) there stand the remains of what appears to have been a large summer palace built by Râjâ Mardan Singh. The most remarkable part of these ruins is a lofty tower to the north of the buildings, which is still standing in tolerable preservation, although some of the lower part of the wall has fallen down. The ground plan of this tower is almost square, each side measuring about 15 feet. It is built in six storeys, each one slightly tapering upwards. The total height is about 100 feet. There is a winding stone staircase the whole way up.

III. 6. **Garhpehra.** Remains of buildings of various kinds.

III. 7. **Itáwá.** Some fine buildings in and close to the town, the stone-work and carvings in which are said to be really remarkable.

III. 8. **Jaisinghnagar,** 21 miles south-west of Sâgar. A fort, in ruins, built by Jâi Singh, the ruler of Garhpehrâ or old Sâgar about 200 years ago.

III. 9. **Kimlasa,** 42 miles north-west of Sâgar. A fort, and a Muhammadan tomb. The walls of the latter are of beautifully perforated screen-work. Also a Hindu *mahál.*

III. 10. **Kurái,** 32 miles north-west of Sâgar. An old fort utilized as a sub-treasury and *tehsil* office.

III. 11. **Madanpur** is situated at the head of one of the principal passes leading from Sâgar to Lalitpur. Site of an old city. There are six temples here, all more or less ruined, the oldest being three Jaina temples to the north of the town. Two others are at the north-west corner of the lake, and the sixth at some distance to the north-east of the lake. Here are several **inscriptions** dating from *Sam.* 1212 to *Sam.* 1692. Also a colossal boar and two inscribed *sati* stones.

III. 12. **Pandalpur.** Temple of Paṇḍharinâtha, where an annual *jatra* is held.

IIa. 13. **Rahatgaḍ,** 25 miles west of Sâgar. Here was a fort which was destroyed in great measure, but the ruins still remain, showing what an enormous structure it was originally. The fort is situated on a lofty eminence to the south-west of the town, and surrounded by it on the south, west, and north sides. It was chiefly built by Sultân Muhammad Khân, but was afterwards altered and added to by his successors, and thus took upwards of fifty years to complete. It is the largest fort in the Sâgar district and probably in all the adjoining country. The outer walls consist of twenty-six enormous towers, some of which were used as dwellings, connected by curtain walls, and enclose a space of sixty-six acres. This space was for the most part covered with buildings of all descriptions, and contained a bâzâr and numerous temples and palaces. One of these latter is called the "Bâdal Mahâl" or Cloud Palace, from its great height and elevated situation. It is attributed to one of the Râj-Gond Chiefs of Garha Mandlâ. Most of the buildings are now in ruins, and the outer fort walls are in a ruinous state. The east wall was breached for a distance of nearly a hundred yards by Sir Hugh Rose's siege guns in 1858, when he captured the fort from the rebels.

III. 14. **Rehli,** 28 miles south-east of Sâgar. A fort built by the Marâthâs about 200 years ago. It stands on the north bank of the Sunâr, opposite to the junction of that river with another small stream called the Dehâr, on a considerable eminence overlooking the town. The space enclosed within it—nearly two acres in extent—was covered with Marâthâ buildings of two or more storeys, most of which have been destroyed.

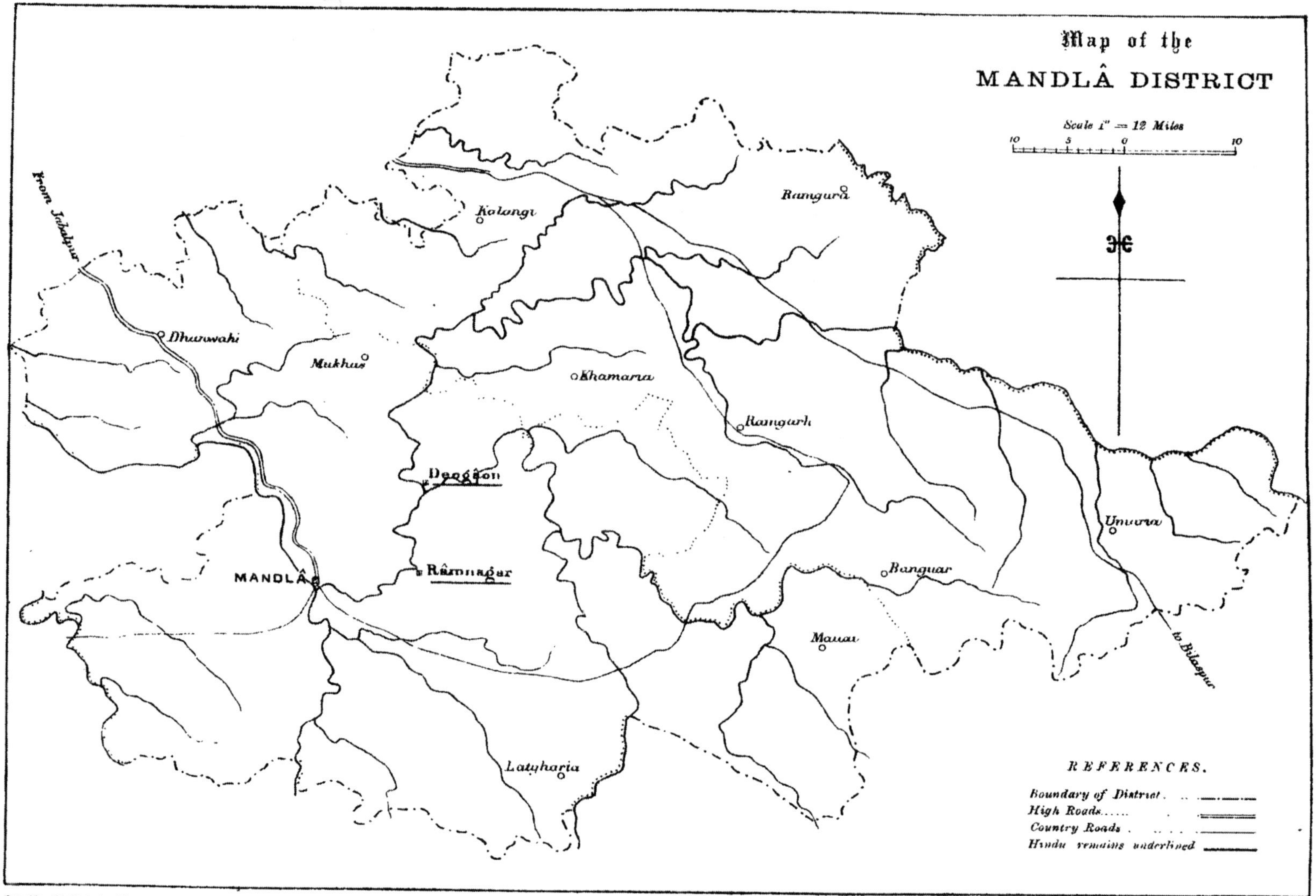
Map of the
MANDLÂ DISTRICT
Scale 1" = 12 Miles
10 5 0 10
From Jabalpur
Dhurowahi
Mukhas
Kolangi
Ramgura
Khamaria
Rangarh
Deogâon
Râmnagar
MANDLÂ
Ranguar
Umaria
to Bilaspur
Mauai
Latyharia
REFERENCES.
Boundary of District
High Roads
Country Roads
Hindu remains underlined

IV.—MANDLÂ.

III. 1. **Mandlá.** A small station on the right bank of the Narmadâ. There is nothing here of much interest, the temples being more or less modern. The old ruined fort is very picturesque but is not a strong fort. The place could never have been of any great importance. (Cunningham's Reports, Vols. VII. and VIII.)

III. 2. **Deogáon,** 20 miles north-east of Mandlâ on the new Dindori road. A very old temple at the junction of the Borhneyr and Narmadâ rivers (*see* Captain Ward's Settlement Report, 1866-69).

III. 3. **Rámnagar,** about 10 miles to the east of Mandlâ. Here are several old Gond palaces but of little architectural merit. Placed in one, however, is the well-
Ia. known **inscription** giving the genealogy of the Râjâs of Mandlâ. (Cunningham's Reports, Vol. VII., p. 106, and Vol. XVII., p. 46.)

V.—Seoni.

III. 1. **Chhapárá,** 22 miles to the north of Seoni on the Jabalpur road. Here the bridge over the Wengangâ is worth inspection, and the remains of the old Gond fort still exist.

III. 2. **Ghansor,** 30 miles north-east of Seoni.* A small village with the ruins of several temples. The ruins extend over an area of about a mile long by a quarter of a mile broad, within this area, on the banks of the little rivulet, which supplies the village with water, are the remains of numerous temples; all the ruins are mere mounds of cut and broken stone, not a single stone standing upon the other. There are the remains of twenty or twenty-five temples, of which only two appear to have been of large size and complete. Beside the temples and a fort are the remains of several tanks. In the village is a fine Jaina statue which is worshipped; there are also a few fragments. About a mile east of the present village, in a *tope* of trees, is a finely carved female statue, and another a short way further east in another *tope.*

II*a*. 3. **Lakhnadon** *tehsil.* There are here collected some good sculptures. Enquiry might be made concerning their former site.

* Another Ghansor is about 70 miles north of Seoni.

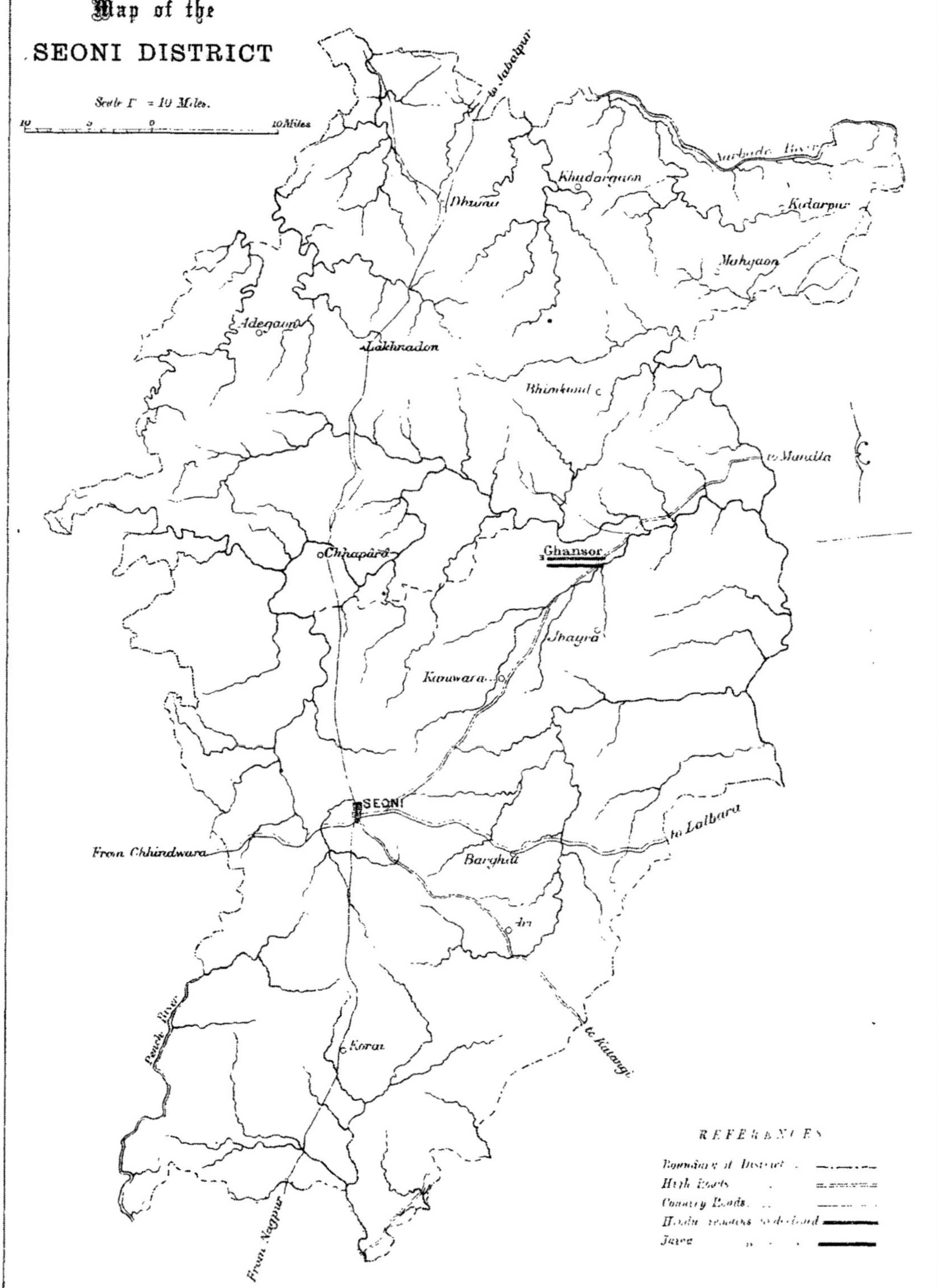
Map of the
SEONI DISTRICT
to Jabalpur
Khudargaon
Dhuma
Mahgaon
Adegaon
Lakhnadon
Chhapara
Ghansor
Jhagra
Kanwara
SEONI
From Chhindwara
to Lalbara
Barghat
Korai
to Katangi
From Nagpur

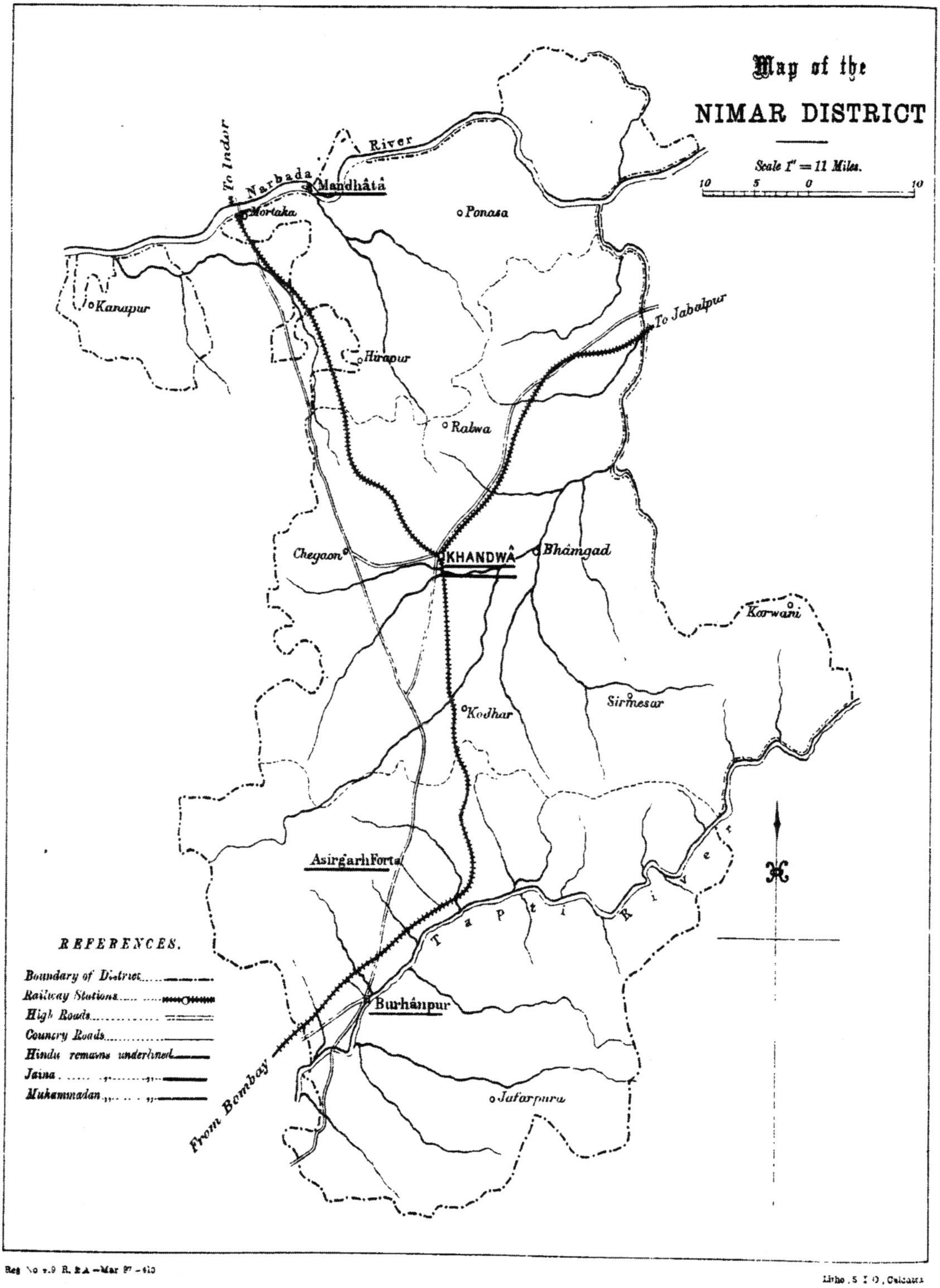

Reg No. 9 R. & A.—Mar 97—410

Litho, S. I. O., Calcutta

III.—NARBADA DIVISION.

I.—NIMÂR.

IIa. 1. **Asirgarh fort.** The construction of this fortress was clearly a work of different periods. The lowest portions of the walls are in similar cyclopean style to those of Mândhâtâ and probably date from about the same period. The place is known to have been held by several dynasties of Râjput rulers, all of whom probably added to, or altered, the fortifications. The columns of an old Jaina temple dug up in the course of some engineering operations would show that it was probably occupied by the same race to whom the ancient buildings at Khandwâ are due. On it are inscribed the names of five princes with the title of Varma, two of whom are stated to have married daughters of the Gupta kings. The character is that usually ascribed to the tenth or eleventh centuries. The upper walls of the fort are evidently of the period when the use of artillery had been introduced, that is of the Muhammadan rule in this part of the country. The outwork called Malligarh is the work of Adil Khân Fârukhi I, about A.D. 1498, who is also stated by Ferishta to have added greatly to the other fortifications. The occurrence of carved stones built into the walls and gateways would show that they were, at least in part, constructed out of the materials of some more ancient buildings. Among the foundations of the fort are many vaulted chambers, now mostly full of water and choked with rubbish, which were probably the old granaries of the fort. In the south-eastern angle is a small shrine of Âsâpûraṇi, the tutelary deity of the Chohan Râjputs who are known to have held the fort in *Samvat* 1351 (A.D. 1294), when it was sacked by Alâu'd-din (Tod's Râjasthân, Vol. II., page 460). The shrine is still attended by the Chohan Râjputs of Piplode, who claim to be the descendants of the old Râjâs of Asîr. The name of the fort may have been derived from Âśâ or Âśâpuraṇi, or perhaps from the ancient title of the Asi or Hihya dynasty of kings who ruled this country from Maheśvara on the Narmadâ, probably about 500 B.C. (Tod's Vol. II., page 442). It is at any rate tolerably sure that Ferishta's etymology of the name from Asa Aheer, whom he states to have held the fort when taken by the Fârukhi of Burhânpur is a fiction, the name Aser being repeatedly mentioned by the Râjput's poet Chânde, and even in the *Mahâbhârata*, where it is said to have become one of the seats of Aśvatthâmâ (a legend still current). There are numerous **inscriptions** on the rocks and buildings of Asîr, which give the dates of its several sieges and of the construction of some of its buildings. Copies and translations of these were made by the Settlement Officer, and some of the most important of them were published by him in the Central Provinces Antiquarian Journal, No. II. The main gateway was built in 1012 H. (A.D. 1611) during the reign of Jahângîr; the mosque (now used as a European barrack) and several of the bastions, in the reign of Shâh Jahân. The great bronze gun on the western bastion was cast at Burhânpur in A.D. 1665 in

Aurangzib's time. A small iron breech-loading gun (1lb. calibre) bears date A.D. 1589, in the time of Ali Khân Fârukhi.

The place was stormed and taken by the army of General Wellesley in the year 1803, made over to Sindia by the treaty of Surji Aryangâon the next year, and again besieged by the British in 1819, its castellan having given shelter to Âpâ Sâheb, the ex-Râjâ of Nâgpur. Since then the fort has remained in British possession. The walls enclose an area of 60 acres and can only be entered from two avenues, the rest of its sides being scarped to a depth of from 80 to 150 feet. It has a never failing water-supply. The fort is 2,200 feet above sea level.

III. 2. **Bhámgaḍ,** 8 miles east of Khandwâ. A fort which was captured and burnt by Yaśavantrâv Shâhi in A.D. 1806.

3. **Burhánpur,** on the north bank of the Tâpti river, 12 miles nearly due south from Asirgarh and 40 miles south-west from Khândwâ. It was founded in A.D. 1399 by Nasir Khân, the first of the Fâruki Kings of Khândesh, on the site of an old Hindu town named Basâna-Khera. It was named Burhânpur in honour of the famous saint Burhânu'd-din of Daulatâbâd. It was the usual residence of all the later Fâruki Kings, and it was during their rule of 200 years that the two great mosques, the Jami and Bibi Masjids were built. The city, within the walls, is just two miles in length from north to south, by half a mile in breadth. But there are numerous remains outside shewing that the suburbs must once have been very extensive. There are several Muhammadan tombs; but the only
IIb. buildings of any archæological interest are the Bibi Masjid and the Jami Masjid.
III. The old waterworks are interesting, many of the old towers connected therewith still existing without the town. Three years ago two of the old water channels were repaired, and the town has thus been furnished with an excellent water supply. (See General Cunningham's Report, Vol. IX., p. 115.)

III. 4. **Khandwá.** The head-quarters town of the Nimâr District. There are numerous remains of Jaina temples scattered about the town of Khandwâ and built into more modern buildings. These remains are to be found very plentifully built into four *kuṇḍas* or tanks in the immediate vicinity of the town called the Râmeśvara Kuṇḍa, the Padma Kuṇḍa, the Bhîma Kuṇḍa, and the Sûrya Kuṇḍa, and constructed of solid masonry. The best specimens of Jaina figures are to be found at Padma Kuṇḍa *bâvali*, in old Khandwâ fort, and the temple of Mahâdeva near Râmeśvara (*see* also Cunningham's Tour, page 113, Vol. IX).

5. **Mándhátá.** On the Narmadâ river, 32 miles north by west from Khandwâ and about seven miles east of Mortakâ railway station. As a Hindu place of pilgrimage Mândhâtâ is famous on account of the presence there of one of the twelve most celebrated *lingas* of Śiva. The town of Mândhâtâ is built partly upon the south bank of the Narmadâ and partly upon an island in the river. The island is, roughly, about a mile and a half long, and is composed of two lofty hills divided by a valley, which runs from near the summit at the eastern end down to the water's edge at the western extremity. These hills join at the eastern end where their sides fall in

precipitous cliffs to the river below, the western ends tailing off gradually. Up the southern face of the south hill is built one-half of the town of Mândhâtâ, and exceedingly picturesque it is with its rows of houses, temples, shops, and the Râjâ's palace, conspicuous above all the rest, all built upon terraces scarped out of the rugged sides of the hill. The rest of the hills are covered with jungle, amongst which are scattered extensive ruins of a much more substantial colony than now exists there. The Narmadâ river, being one of the most sacred rivers of India, is crowded with *jogis* and pilgrims, many of whom do the *pradakshiṇá* of the river—that is, they start from Broach and travel along its north bank to its source among the hills at Amarakanṭak and return again to Broach by the southern bank. This is said to take three years to accomplish, but this includes all the halts at the numberless sacred spots along its banks.

Upon the tops of the hills forming the island of Mândhâtâ are signs of a once flourishing settlement, and temples, basements, long lines of walling, fortifications, and gateways, in most part in ruin, shew that the place was once of no small importance. But this is now, save for a little attention to one or two of the shrines, practically deserted, and stands high above, and apart from the modern town. Among the ruins are some fine old temples and other buildings. The town with its scores of comparatively modern temples is not so interesting. The great columns in
III. the temple of Oṁkâra are certainly old, and belong to a former structure, the present building being of no great age. A curious arrangement in it is that the *linga* cell is not placed, as is usual, in the line with the front door of the temple, but is placed to one side, so that the *linga* cannot be seen except from the remote inner end of the hall.

Ib. The temple of Siddhanâtha, upon the top of the hill, now in ruins, is the principal and most interesting relic of antiquity at Màndhâtâ. It stands upon the plateau towards the eastern edge, upon a raised platform whose plinth is supported all around by elephants in various positions in relief, two of which have found their way to the Museum at Nâgpur, where they guard the entrance to that building. The central shrine still stands with its four entrances, one on each of its four sides, and the great columns of the four porches. The *śikhara* or spire of the shrine and the roofs of the porches have fallen. The temple has been well decorated.

III. Among the other ruins on the hill is a large bracketted gateway similar to, though not so elaborate as to those at Dabhoi in Gujarât. It is in a very ruinous condition.
IIb. It is one of the gateways of the old fort. Of another old temple the shrine and tower remain with a very large *linga* within. The plan is star-shaped, formed by the corners of superimposed squares. There are also the ruins of other temples, together with a Vaishṇava shrine still in use at the western end of the plateau. Ruined walls and basements of houses, together with loose sculptures, shew that an extensive settlement once existed here.

II.—Hoshangâbâd.

III. 1. **Bágrá,** on the Tawâ river. A small fortress and a *dargâh* in honour of Sultân Hoshang Shâh Ghori, one of the Mâlwa kings.

III. 2. **Charwa,** 73 miles south-west of Hoshangâbâd and 4 miles from Khirkian railway station. A fort.

III. 3. **Joga,** 24 miles from Hardâ railway station. A fort, said to have been built by Sultân Hoshang Shâh Ghori. There is a tomb here (Mr. Elliott's Settlement Report, pp. 21 and 22).

III. 4. **Kalibhit,** 36 miles south of Harda. A fortress in a ruinous state.

III. 5. **Khatama,** 21 miles south of Hoshangâbâd, and about 10 miles from Itârsi railway station. A cave dedicated to Mahâdeva. It consists of a plain rectangular room in the end of which stands an enclosed shrine, leaving a *pradakshiṇá* around it and between it and the wall of the cave, while before the shrine, and supporting the forward part of the cave, are four columns.

II*a*. 6. **Pachmarhi,** about 32 miles south of Piparia railway station. The hot weather hill station for the Central Provinces. Here there is a series of plain neatly cut caves in a hillock to the south-east of the station. There is nothing in them to indicate with any degree of certainty to what religion they originally belonged.

III. 7. **Sohágpur,** 32 miles east of Hoshangâbâd. Said to be Sonitpura to which Munja, the brother of Bhoja Râjâ, transferred the seat of government from Ujjain: a colossal statue was discovered here (Tr. L. S. Bom. III., 536).

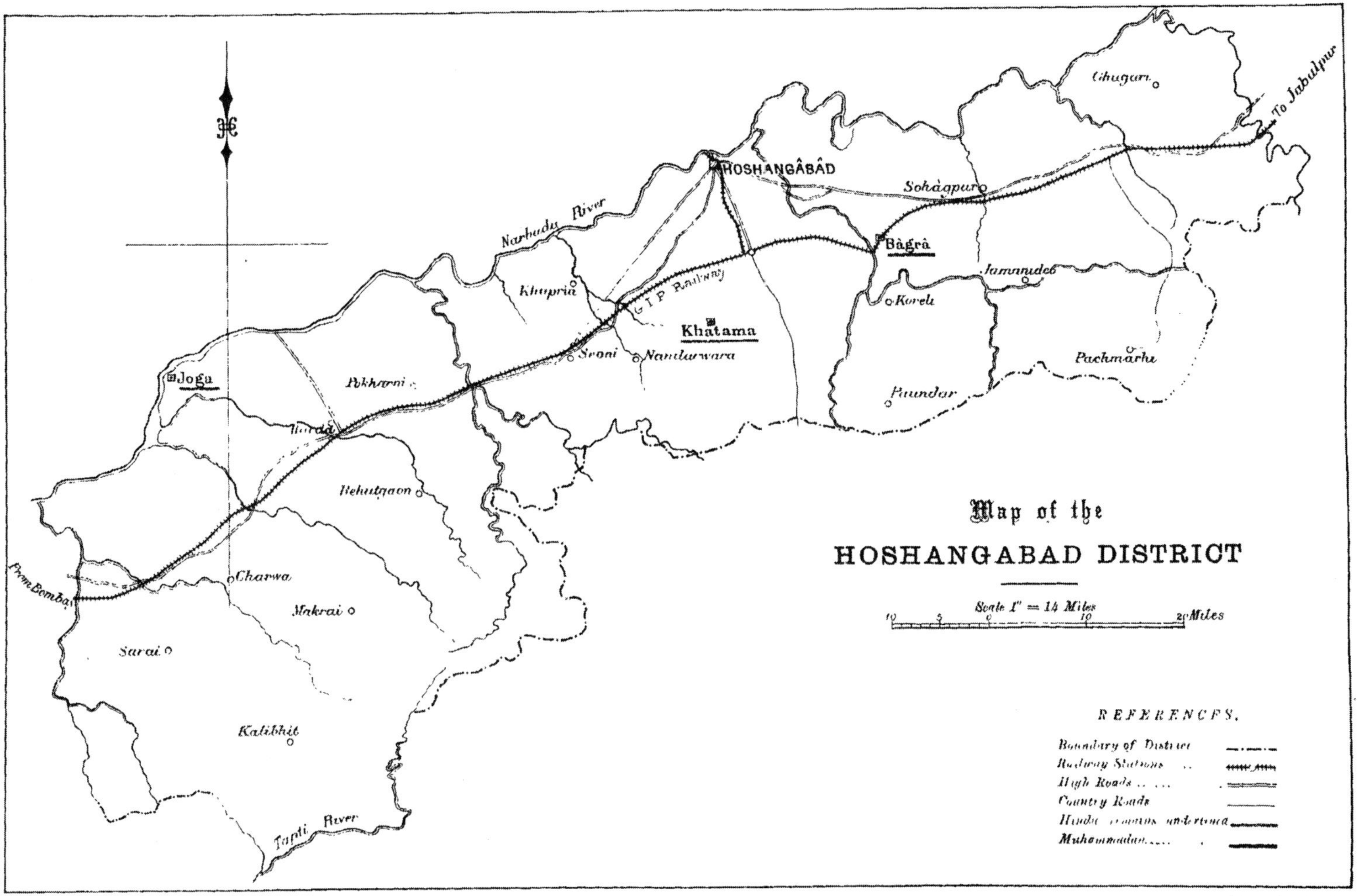

Reg No 419 R & A —Mar 97.—410

Litho, S. I. O., Calcutta

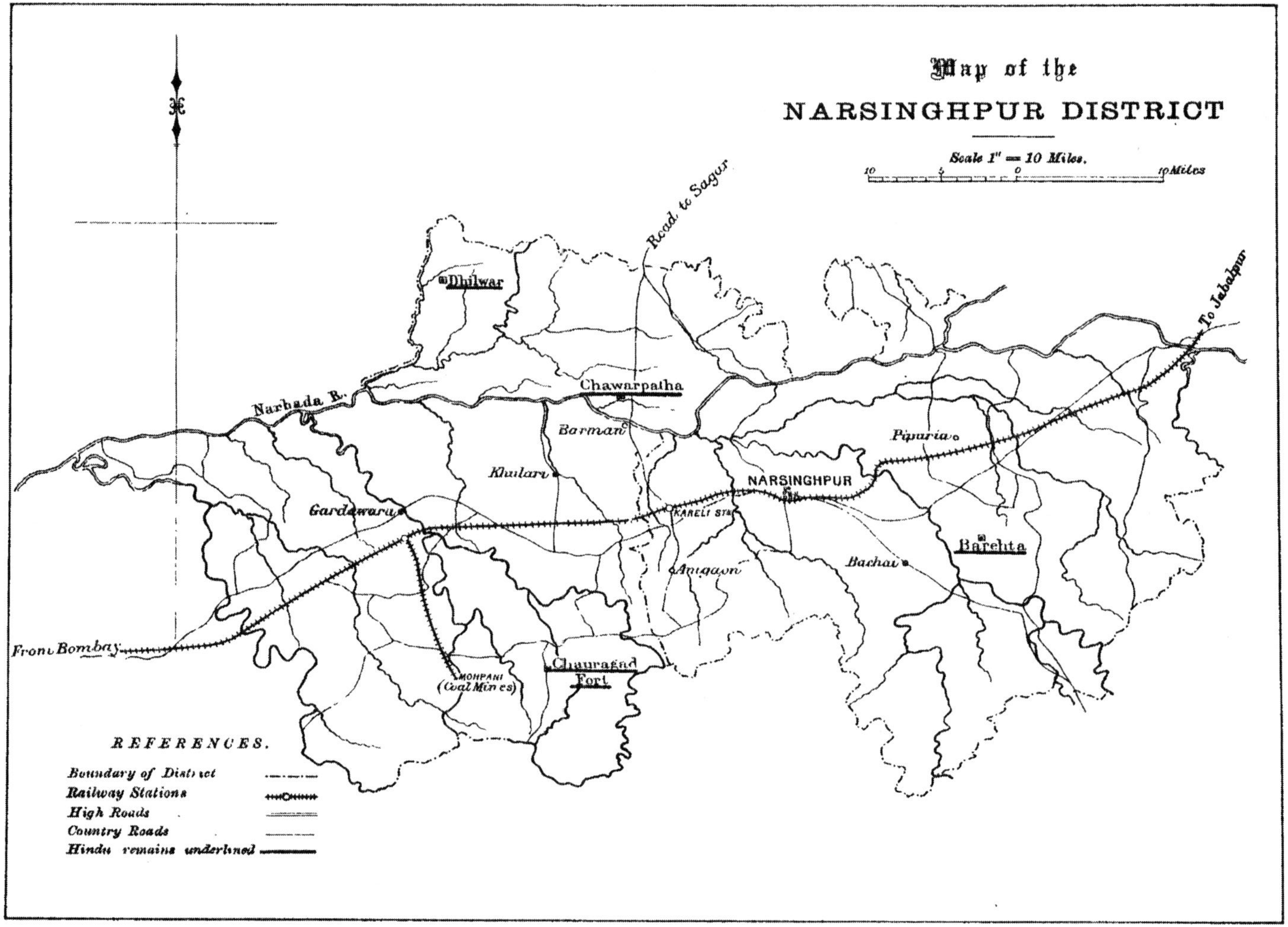

Red No 419. R & A—Feb 97—410

Litho. S I O, Calcutta.

III.—Narsinghpur.

Ia. 1. **Narsinghpur.** In the public garden at Narsinghpur there are some very interesting sculptures which were collected by Colonel Bloomfield from various parts of the district. Most of them were brought from Barehtâ. They shew that there once existed in this district a high class of old temples. The district is now, however, practically barren, the railway, running as it does through the whole length of it, having absorbed a great deal of what remained up to that time in its construction.

The sculptures in the garden consist of pillars, doorways, portions of the same, beams, and figures, together with some old guns. Most interesting of all, perhaps, is a very complete and elaborately carved doorway which is set up across a pathway, and is, with the exception of the dedicatory block upon the lintel, in a thorough good state of preservation. The dedicatory block has sufficient of the figures upon it to shew that they were Vishṇu and Lakshmi seated upon Garuda.

III. 2. **Barehtá,** 14 miles to the south-east of Narsinghpur. Barehtâ has evidences of great antiquity, but its remains have been much harried by railway contractors. The best of its sculptures are believed to be in Berlin and Warsaw. Now nothing remains but a little walled enclosure with a few figures placed within it.

III. 3. **Barman,** on the side of the road which leads from Kareli railway station to Sâgar. A fine old *bâvali.*

III. 4. **Chauragaḍ** fort, about 20 miles to the south-west of Narsinghpur. This fort was the great stronghold and citadel of the Gond kingdom and witnessed every crisis in its history.

III. 5. **Chawarpatha,** 14 miles north-west of Narsinghpur. The remains of a Gond fort. The gateway, part of the wall and a bastion are still standing, and are in a fairly good state of preservation.

III. 6. **Dhilwar,** in the north-west corner of the district. Remains of a Gond fort in fair state of preservation, also a picturesque *bâvali* in a good state of preservation.

IV.—Betul.

III. 1. **Badnur,** the head-quarters of the Betul district. Not far from Badnur is Kherlâ, the former residence of the Gond Râjâs, where there is an old fort, now in ruins, which used to be held by them.

III. 2. **Betul.** There is an old fort here.

III. 3. **Akhalvárá.** A *masjid* and a *bávali.*

III. 4. **Amla,** about 18 miles from Badnur on the Chhindwârâ road. Some old tombs, said to be those of Gond kings.

III. 5. **Asirgaḍ Fort.** It is in a ruinous state. An old gun is lying upon it.

III. 6. **Atner,** two cisterns called *tapatjhiras.*

III. 7. **Badegáon.** Some old temples situated on the bank of the Tâpti.

II*b*. 8. **Bhesdehi.** Two *kuṇḍas* called *tapatjhiras,* and an old temple with fine stone carving. The entrance of the temple and a part of the façade and pillars are still standing, and the carving in many parts is still wonderfully clear, though probably not much under three hundred years old. Additions have been made to the original structure, as is shewn by the introduction of palpable obscenities into some of the carvings, the majority of which are quite free from any such objectionable subjects. A large *pipal* tree has grown out of the rear of the building and displaced large portions of the masonry. There is also a fort.

III. 9. **Bhopali.** An old cave-temple of Mahâdeva in a hill. A fair is held here at *Sivarâtri.*

III. 10. **Bori.** A cistern situated near the village.

III. 11. **Borpend,** an old temple situated in the jungle.

III. 12. **Chawal,** a stone temple.

III. 13. **Chichthána,** images of "Bârâlingas" lie on the bank of the Tâpti.

III. 14. **Dagdaga Bhandarpani.** An image called "Killangdeva."

III. 15. **Dhaba.** A *masjid* said to have been built by the Emperor Alamgir.

III. 16. **Dhanora.** There is here a deep waterfall in the Tâpti, and situated in the opposite hill is a cave.

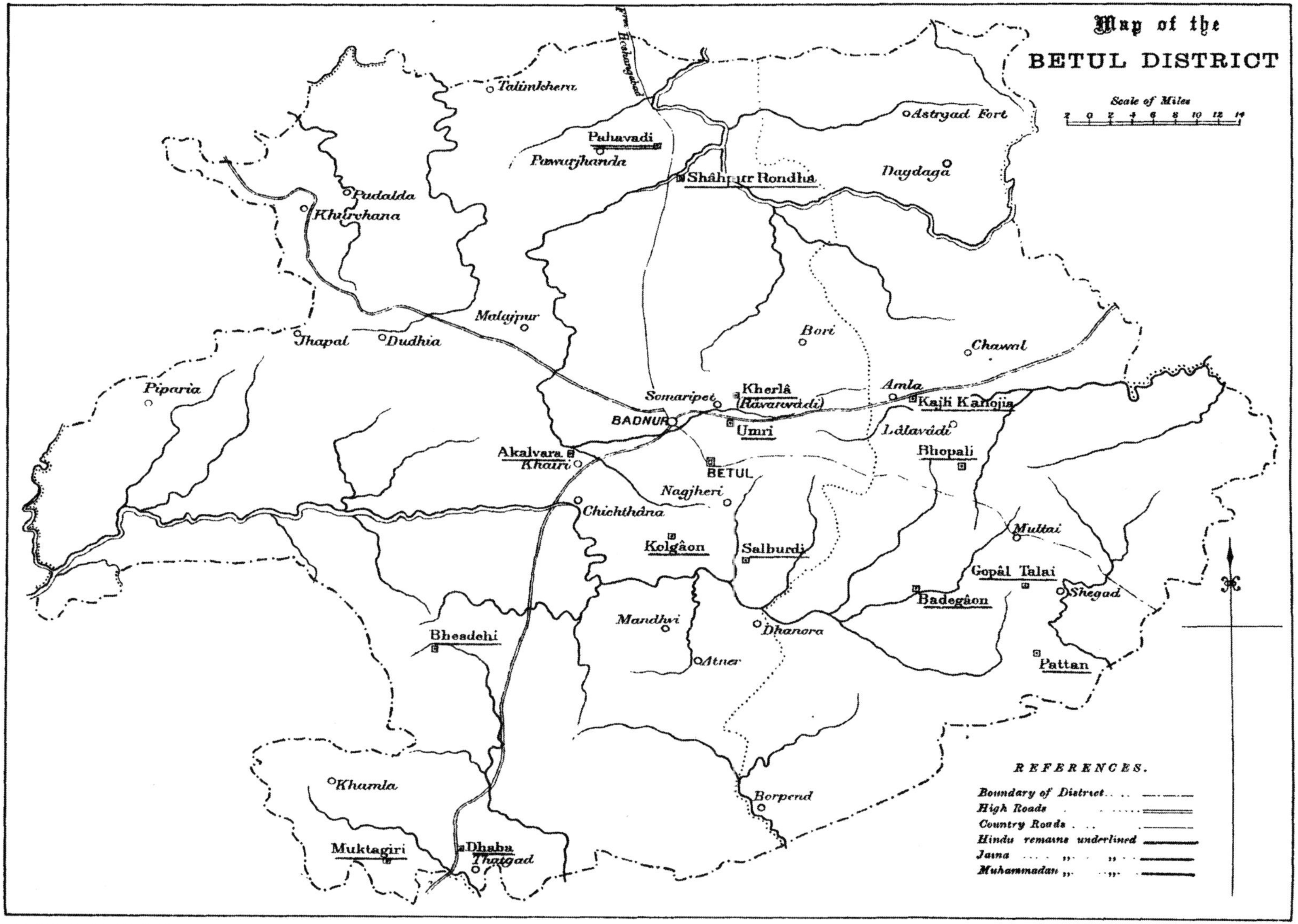

Reg. No 419, R & A.—Mar 97—410

Litho., S I O, Calcutta

III. 17. **Dudhia.** Several stone images of horsemen.

III. 18. **Gopál Talái.** A tomb of Rehman Shâh Dullâh, but apparently of not much account.

III. 19. **Jhapàl.** A cave called "Tâpsibovâki Kho."

III. 20. **Kajli Kanojia.** There are stone images lying near the village. On the banks of the Bel river there are ruins of old temples. It is said that two masons, named Nangar and Bhongar used to work at the images in a state of nudity in an enclosure surrounded with walls. They had ordered their sisters to give them previous warning before they entered the enclosure whenever they carried food for them. One day the sisters entered the enclosure without previous warning and found the brothers quite naked. Both the brothers and their sisters were instantly transformed into stone figures. This is supposed to account for naked images found there. Some figures were recently sent to the Residency at Nâgpur from this place. Probably Jaina statues.

Mr. Palmer, Executive Engineer, a short while ago brought to notice the existence of some very interesting remains at Kanojia near Amla on the Badnur-Chhindwârâ road.

III. 21. **Khairi.** Five caves and a cistern situated in the hill close to a place called "Mahâdeva."

III. 22. **Khamla.** An old fort.

III. 23. **Kherlá.** A fort and two tanks. People say that Râjâ Il used to live in the fort. Within the fort is the temple of Mukundaràja Svâmi, a celebrated Hindu saint. It is said that Râjâ Jailpâla used to imprison every saint who failed to shew him the god. In this way he had incarcerated about three hundred. He used to demand of each that he should shew him the god in as little time as was necessary for a man to put his foot in the stirrup. Mukundarâja heard of this, came to Kherla, shewed the god to Jailpâla and liberated all the saints.

Of the two tanks, one is in the fort while the other is about a mile from it.

III. 24. **Khurchana.** A fort called Sâvaligaḍ. Upon this fort there are seven cisterns containing fresh water—natural springs. The cisterns have been cut in hard black stone. An old *jogi* used to live here.

III. 25. **Kolgáon.** A *masjid* said to have been built by Alamgir.

III. 26. **Lálavádi.** A cave situated in the hills. People say that Nangar and Bhongar used to live there.

III. 27. **Malajpur.** A tomb of Guru Sâheb, where a fair is held in December and an old well called Chakabo, said to have been built by a dancing girl.

III. 28. **Mandhvi.** A *táká* or cistern belonging to a goddess. There is a stone here which sounds like iron when struck.

III. 29. **Muktagiri,** in Betul to the north of Elichpur. A collection of modern Jaina temples of no particular interest, and possessing few or no architectural features worthy of note. They form, however, a very picturesque group, perched upon the precipitous ledges of rock at the end of a secluded and wild ravine, where a pretty waterfall comes tumbling down to the valley from the highlands above.

III. 30. **Multái.** A tank from which the river Tâpti takes its rise. Situated near the *kuṇḍa* is an old inscription upon stone.

III. 31. **Nágjheri.** Situated in a hill is a cave.

III. 32. **Padaldá.** In the jungle between Padaldâ and Pipariâ are two temples called Râni Kho.

III. 33. **Pahavádi.** Some very old temples, a *masjid*, and a *bávali* or well.

III. 34. **Pattan.** A *dargáh* of Sulimân Shâh. Here the well known Sulimân *mankas* (beads) are found.

III. 35. **Pipariá,** *see* Padalda.

III. 36. **Powarjhanda.** An old fort called Bhowargaḍ; it is in a ruinous condition. On its top there is a tank and some cisterns having natural springs.

III. 37. **Rávanvádi.** An old *masjid.*

III. 38. **Sálburdi.** A cave and two cisterns. One cistern contains cold and the other warm water.

III. 39. **Sháhpur Rondha,** a temple in which is a large iron *trisúla.*

II*a*. 40. **Shegaḍ.** A fort with two fine gateways.

III. 41. **Somaripet.** A stone inscription lies in the jungle the letters of which cannot be deciphered.

III. 42. **Talimkhera.** A spring and a *kuṇḍa* or cistern.

III. 43. **Thatgaḍ.** An old fort.

III. 44. **Umri.** The tomb of Rehmân Shâh.

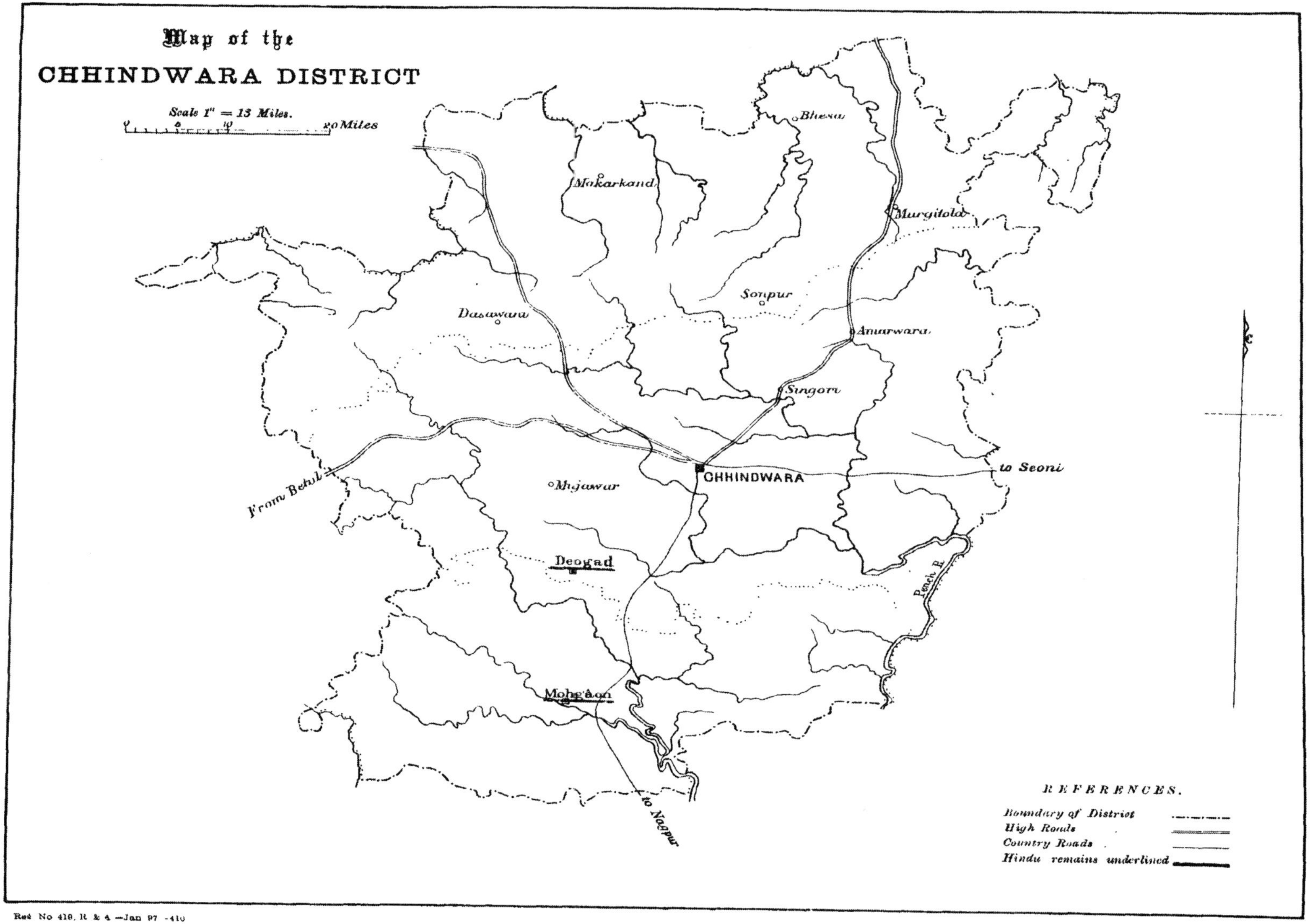

Red No 419, R & 4 —Jan 97 -410

Litho, S I O, Calcutta.

V.—Chhindwârâ.

III. 1. **Deogaḍ.** A village situated in the hills about 24 miles south-west of Chhindwârâ.

Deogaḍ was formerly the seat of the ancient Gond Râjâ who ruled over this country. Bukht Buland, a contemporary of Aurangzib, is said to have resided chiefly at Deogaḍ, and during his time the country over which he ruled and which formed the mid-land Gond kingdom is said to have been in a very flourishing condition. His successor Chand Sultân transferred his residence to Nâgpur, which he subsequently made his capital. Even previous to the period of the Gond Râjâs, tradition points to a Gavali dynasty having been seated at Deogaḍ, but the early history of this dynasty is much wrapped up in obscurity.

The village at present consists of only fifty or sixty houses, but foundations can be traced, in what is now jungle, for a considerable distance round. These with the numerous remains of wells, tanks, etc., shew that the former city must have extended over a very large area. There are also several old temples and the ruins of a fine stone fort. The whole of the buildings are constructed of the finest limestone. The situation of Deogaḍ is extremely picturesque.

III. 2. **Mohgâon.** A municipal town on a tributary of the river Jâm, 38 miles south of Chhindwârâ. On either side of the river is a large Hindu temple, one of which, sacred to Mahâdeva, is said to be three centuries old.

IV.—CHHATTISGAḌ DIVISION.

I.—RÂIPUR.

III. 1. **Râipur** itself does not boast of any very ancient building. The fort is acknowledged to be the most ancient. Within the fort are numerous temples; some of these, though of little interest, are worth noticing only for their negative value. The temples of Râipur are to be counted by the score, but all of much the same type. The unfinished temple of Dudhadhâri Mâtâ, as an instance of modern elaborate carving, is probably unrivalled in the Central Provinces; but this beautiful building is disfigured by sculpture of the most indecent type, executed in stucco on its exterior, and alone, of all other sculptures, as if especially to attract attention, gaudily coloured. In the courtyard of the temple are gathered a number of fragments, said to have been brought from Śirpur; these fragments are of special interest; they are well executed, and prove that Buddhism and Jainism flourished in Śirpur.

The museum at Râipur contains a few **inscriptions**; two of these are from Śirpur. A third is on a *sati* pillar from Simgâ. (General Cunningham's Reports, Vol. VII., p. 165.)

IIb. 2. **Ârang**, 24 miles east of Râipur. Here there are many fine old tanks all around, with numerous remains of temples and sculptures which are chiefly Brahmanical. The only temple that is now standing is a Jaina one, and this would probably have fallen some time ago, had it not been held together by two iron bands, which the surveyors put around it when they used it as a survey station. Half a mile further to the east is the Bâgeśvara temple, which is visited by all the pilgrims on their way to Jagannâtha. To the west of the town, on the bank of the Mahâmâyâ tank, there is a small temple dedicated to the Mahâmâyâ or "Great Mother." Many fragments of sculpture are collected here, with a broken **inscription** slab containing 18 lines of writing. Inside the enclosure there are two naked Jaina figures half life-size. A second tank, called the Nârâyana Tâl lies to the west of the Mahâmâyâ tank from which it is only separated by an embankment. On its banks are many life-size statues of Vishṇu with numerous squared stones of large dimensions, the remains of some ancient temple. Foundations and pillar bases are found when digging for bricks. In 1881, General Cunningham found, among the rough flat stones collected near the Police station, a slab bearing two short **inscriptions** in the old characters found on the Amarâvati *stûpas*. Ârang has all the appearance of having once been a very large city. (General Cunningham's Reports, Vol. XVII., p. 20). In addition to the above Mr. Beglar, in Report, Vol.

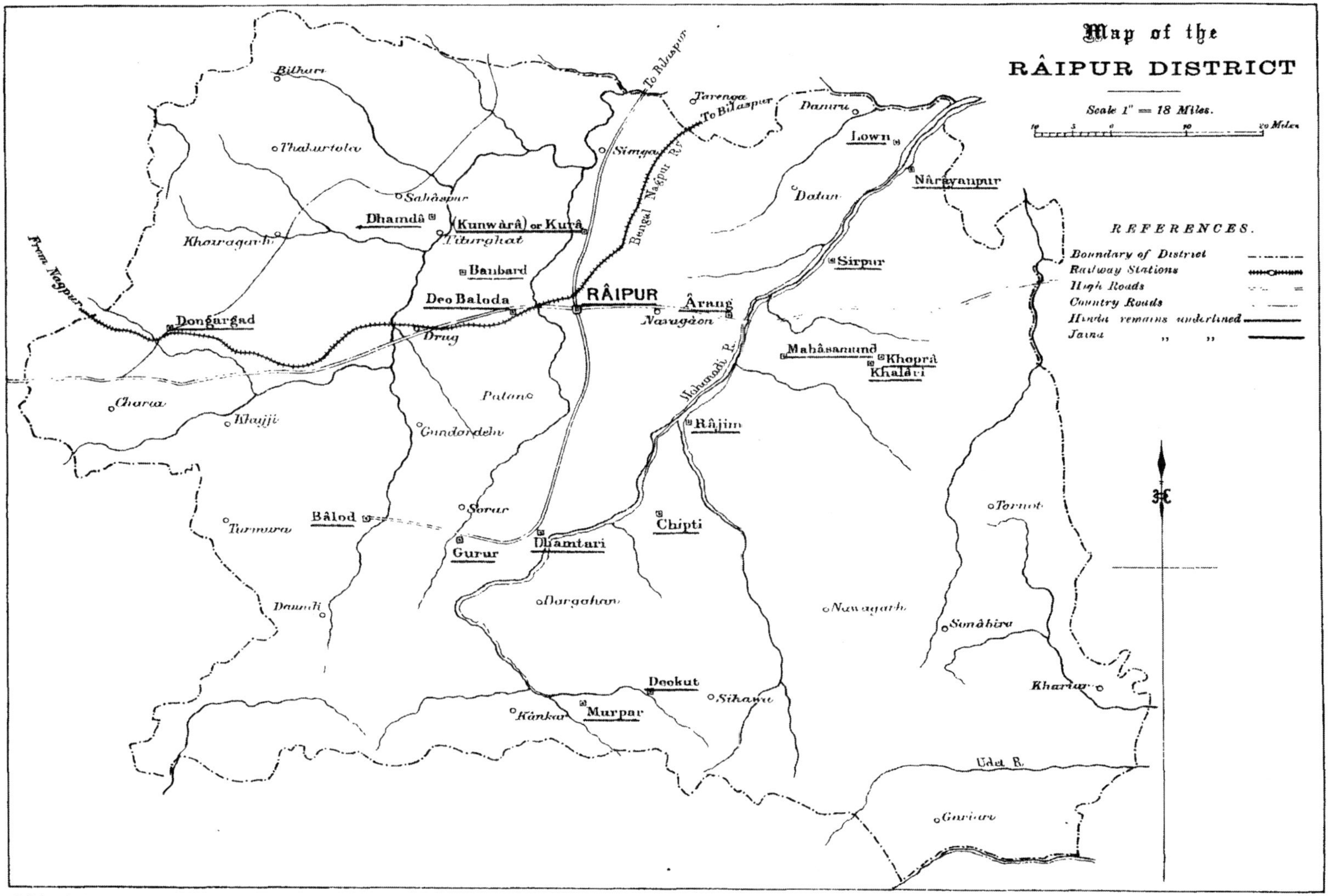

Reg. No 410, R & A—Jan 07—410

Litho S. I. O., Calcutta

VII., p. 160, mentions another very elaborately carved, but grossly indecent temple called the Bhand *deval.*

III. 3. **Bálod,** 44 miles south-west of Râipur, possesses numerous temples and a ruined fort. At the east end of the city, and to the north of the road, which likewise marks the customs line, are several old temples. One group consists of seven temples, of which two are quite modern, built of the fragments of older ones. To the west of the group of temples is a large tank now almost dry, and traces of another beyond. Two other tanks exist a few hundred yards to the south-west, and another to the south: this last is now quite filled up. *Sati* pillars are very numerous here, on the banks of all tanks in the village and the fort; the most
IIa. interesting of these is on the road-side, about half a mile to the east of the city. This pillar has served three times already as a *sati* monument. It has three **inscriptions,** but the dates in the first two are partly worn away. The third inscription is "in three lines, in characters which Prinsep ascribes to the second century A.D." (Cunningham's Reports, Vol. VII., p. 133.)

III. 4. **Banbard,** in Drug *tehsil.* Remains of old buildings are seen about, and a temple dedicated to Râmachandra. The place is generally called Papharan.

III. 5. **Belars,** in the Sahâspur *zamindari.* The remains of a temple which is said to have been built during the reign of Vrashakuvar Râjâ.

III. 6. **Chhind Kharak,** in Kânkar State. A fort built in *Samvat* 1189.

IIb. 7. **Chipti** of Dhamtari. Temples of Mahâdeva and Râmachandra. An **inscription** shews that Râjâ Mâldeva constructed the temples about 700 years ago, while he was ruling over Dhamtari and Kankar territory.

III. 8. **Damru** in Simgâ *tehsil,* 9 miles north-west of Lown. An old temple.

IIb. 9. **Deo Baloda,** a small village 12 miles to the west of Râipur. It possesses an old sandstone temple which is said to be similar to one of the temples at Ârang. This temple is dedicated to Śiva. The outside of the shrine is decorated with some quaint sculptures. The four central pillars of the *maṇḍapa* are very richly moulded, and are highly polished. (General Cunningham's Reports, Vol. XVII., p. 4.)

III. 10. **Deokut,** 8 miles west of Sihawa. Four small but old temples on the banks of the river. In two other temples are very elaborate carved slabs. (General Cunningham's Reports, Vol. VII., p. 146.)

III. 11. **Dhamdá** in Drug *tehsil.* Gateway of the old fort which was constructed during the time of Râjâ Dasvant Singh of Dhamdâ.

III. 12. **Dhamtari,** 36 miles south of Râipur. Here are numerous tanks which in numbers, size, and height of embankments form quite a feature of the place.

There are near the southern end of the city several temples, all close to each other and to the modern Government dispensary. These are more or less uninteresting being late, although apparently rebuilt of older material. There is one exception, a small but elegant temple near the dispensary which would seem to date back to much earlier times. (General Cunningham's Reports, Vol. VII., p. 142.)

III. 13. **Dongargaḍ** in the Khairagaḍ State, 56 miles due west of Râipur. "Dongargaḍ is situated in a basin of the hills surrounded by jungle, and is supposed to occupy a portion of the site of the ancient city of Kâmantipura. Within the last 40 years (now 60) six old world temples stood here; but in the time of the late ruler of Nâgpur, these were knocked down, and their materials used for the construction of bridges on the former Nâgpur and Râipur road. Within a small radius from Dongargaḍ there are numerous ruined tanks, and for miles around, in what is now jungle, there are remains of old foundations, built of strong massive bricks, specimens of which were recently sent to the Nâgpur museum." (From account by Colonel Lucie Smith in Cunningham's Report, Vol. XVII., p. 2.) Ruins of a temple called Girologaḍ. Local enquiry shews that this temple was dedicated to the hill god named Seb Gundi, whose image still exists on the top of the hill.

III. 14. **Drug** is an old town, with a fort on the eastern bank of the Seonâth river, 24 miles to the west of Râipur. It is situated on the high road leading from Nâgpur through Râipur to the eastward, and must have been a place of some consequence for several centuries. At Anjora, on a high mound 4 miles to the west of Drug, there is a figure about 2½ feet high. At Drug itself there is also a small figure of Buddha without a head, and numerous stone foot stools. These stools are generally about 12 inches long and 6 inches high, with four small feet. (Cunningham's Reports, Vol. XVII., p. 3.)

III. 15. **Gurur,** a small village 13 miles east by south of Bâlod. Near the village are the remains of numerous temples. To the north-west of the village is a large tank, close to which is a temple. Five hundred feet to the north of this are the ruins of another temple. (Cunningham's Reports, Vol. VII., pp. 138 and 142.)

III. 16. **Kánker,** head-quarters of the Kânker Feudatory State, 67 miles south by west from Râipur. A fort and some very curious old temples to the west of the village. One has a *bîjak* or **inscription**, giving, it seems, some particulars of its history. (Cunningham's Reports, Vol. VII., p. 147.)

III. 17. **Karaf** in Kânker. A temple said to have been built some 700 or 800 years ago.

III. 18. **Khalári,** thirty miles north-east of Râjim known usually as Khartti Khalâri. Here are several temples, the principal one of which stands on the edge of a small dirty pool in the quarter of the city known as the *killá*. The temple is Śaivic, and has a figure of Gaṇapati over the entrance. It is particularly devoid of sculptured ornament. In a smaller temple, built into the wall of the *maṇḍapa* is an interesting inscription dated *Samvat* 1470. There are the ruins of two other temples to the east of the village.

III. 19. **Khariar**, head-quarters of the Khariar State. The remains of an ancient fort and building. This was the seat of the Ganja-Bansi Râjâs.

III. 20. **Khoprá** is a small dome-shaped bare rock about a mile and a half or two miles east of Khalâri. The sister of Khalâri Mâtâ is said to live there; her name is Khoprâ. A few fragments of pillars, some elaborately sculptured, lie in the village, and a few *sati* pillars are to be met with in the scrub jungle about the village. (Cunningham's Reports, Vol. VII., p. 158.)

III. 21. **Kunwárá**, Kurâ, or Kurira, is situated 14 miles to the north of Râipur. Its foundation is attributed to Râjâ Kunvat, and a large tank is assigned to his Queen as the Râni Talâv. Like most old places Kunwârâ is surrounded by numerous tanks. To the south there is a group of four small stone temples on the banks of the Michni Tank, all of which have lost their entrance porticoes. There were formerly several other and much larger temples in the village, especially two Jaina temples. These were given up by Khub-chand Bania (a Jain) to Mr. Read, the Deputy Commissioner, and were dismantled by Muhammad Yakub, Overseer, to make the causeway across the bed of the Kulhân river, near which there are several carved stones now lying. The stone steps of two tanks, named Dâni Tâl and Bhor Tál, were also taken for the same purpose. Even the pillars were carried off, but some statues were left behind which are now lying about the village. According to Khub-chand himself, three temples in the village were pulled down, as well as the two Jaina temples at Mâlkam. To the west of the village is a ruined temple 18½ feet square with a figure of Śiva still standing inside. There are also several *sati* stones at Kunwârâ, of which one, under a tamarind tree, is certainly old. (Cunningham's Reports, Vol. XVII., p. 31.) Kurâ (Kunwârâ) contains five or six temples, one of them said to have its roof covered with an inscription in *Nágari* characters. (Cunningham's Reports, Vol. VII., p. 168.)

III. 22. **Lown** in Simgâ *tehsil* has a modern temple whose pillars are monoliths and may have been brought from some other temple. Also the ruins of a *mahál* built during the time of the Hai Hai Bansi dynasty.

III. 23. **Mahásamund**, 10 miles north-west of Khalâri. Two temples built of coarse granite and laterite, dedicated to Śiva. A few fragments, chiefly of Gaṇeśa, lie scattered in and about the village. The temples are built without mortar in a plain massive style. (Cunningham's Reports, Vol. VII., p. 159.)

24. **Málkam**, *see* Kunwârâ.

III. 25. **Mundpái** in Kânker State, temples said to be 700 or 800 years old.

III. 26. **Murpar**, 10 miles west from Deokuṭ. Some curious old ruined temples; and some images of Mahâdeva, Gaṇeśa, Râmachandra and Vishṇu. (Cunningham's Reports, Vol. VII., p. 147.)

IIb. 27. **Nárâyanpur**, 53 miles north-east by east of Râipur, on the Mahânadi, some old stone temples, the principal one of which is richly adorned with bold mouldings and a profusion of sculpture. It contains numerous well executed statues. The temple was Śaivic. A few other small shrines exist in the vicinity. To the south of the village are traces of buildings, probably temples. (Cunningham's Reports, Vol. VII., p. 193.)

III. 28. **Navagáon** is an old village on the high road between Ârang and Râipur. It possesses a fine tank called Deora Tâl, on the eastern embankment of which stands a group of temples. There are two stone temples and two brick temples. The two stone temples appear to have been built from the materials of an older temple. (Cunningham's Reports, Vol. XVII., p. 22.)

III. 29. **Old Road.** The line of one of the most important roads of ancient times may be traced through this part of the country. It appears to have come from some point near Bhâṇḍak or Devalvârâ, supposed to be the ancient Kuṇḍilpur, through Deotek close past Palâsgaḍ, past Banjâri (a great mart for articles of traffic by pack animals), past Ambâgaḍ Chauki (which possesses a small fort of no interest, and probably not very old), past Bâlod, Sorar, to Gurur, whence it branched into two, one going *viá* Kânker and Sihawa towards Ganjâm, through the great fort of Jaugaḍ, which contains one of Aśoka's edicts, the other branch going past Dhamtari and Râjim, thence probably skirting the Mahânadi northwards past Sabaripura, Seorinârâyan, etc., to Katak.

Ib. 30. **Rájim**, 24 miles south-east of Râipur. The most holy place in Mahâ-Kosala is Râjim, with its fine group of temples dedicated to Vishṇu. The principal temple of Râjiva-lochana is visited by thousands of pilgrims on their way to Jagannâtha in Orissa. They come to pay their devotions to Râmachandra, whose statue is said to be enshrined inside. But the figure is actually one of the common four-armed representations of Vishṇu himself, with his usual symbols of the club, the discus, the shell, and the lotus. The title of Râjîva-lochana, or the "lotus-eyed" belongs to Râma but not to Vishṇu, and is therefore, presumably, not so old as the temple itself, which was certainly dedicated to Vishṇu. There are two old inscriptions inside the temple, engraved in characters of very different ages; one is dated *Chedi Samvat* 896 (A.D. 1145), while the other seems to be at least three centuries older.

The temples of Râjim, with one exception, form a single group of buildings clustered round the holy shrine of Râjîva-lochana. The group comprises the following temples:—

1. Râjîva-lochana, or Râjib-lochan.
2. Varâha — at the four corners of the courtyard of the above.
3. Narasinha — at the four corners of the courtyard of the above.
4. Badarinâtha — at the four corners of the courtyard of the above.
5. Vâmana — at the four corners of the courtyard of the above.
6. Râjesvara to the west.
7. Dânesvara to the south-west.
8. Jagannâtha to the north-west.

With the two exceptions of the Râjeśvara and Dâneśvara *lingam* shrines, the whole of these temples are dedicated to the worship of Vishṇu.

IIb. (1) Temple of Râjîva-lochana. This fine building, 59 feet in length by 25½ feet in breadth, rises from a platform 69 feet in length by 43 feet in breadth, with a height of 8 feet. The *maṇḍapa*, or hall, is 37 feet 9 inches in length from north to south, by 17 feet in breadth, and is open only at the northern end. There are two flights of steps at the north-west and south-west corners of the platform leading into the western end of the hall, through two side doors. At the east end of the hall, there is the usual small *antarâla*, or ante-chamber, leading into the sanctuary, which, as usual, is nearly quite dark. The flat roof of the hall is supported on two rows of six pillars each down the middle, and a single row of six pilasters on either side. The pillars are square, the lower half being quite plain, and the upper half highly ornamented. But the twelve side pilasters are each ornamented with a tall single figure sculptured on the face, after the fashion of the pillars of a Buddhist *stûpa* railing.

The spire of the sanctum is a square pyramid with carved sides. It is divided into five stages or rows of niches with corrugated pinacles at the corners, very much of the style of the great Mahâbodhi temple at Buddha Gayâ. The base of the sanctum is 20 feet square outside.

The courtyard of the temple is 147 feet in length from east to west, by 102 feet in width. The principal entrance is on the west side, but there is a small doorway or postern on the east side. The main entrance is itself a highly ornamented structure, with pillars and pilasters on both fronts of the doorway, both inside and outside, forming two open chambers. In the two corners of the inner chamber are two figures, one a rude stone, coloured red, which has once been a statue of Hanumân, the other a black stone statue of Buddha, with the usual curly hair, sitting in contemplation under the Bodhi tree, with his right hand resting on his knee and his left hand on his lap. The ears are pierced and elongated after the usual Buddhist fashion. It is not fixed in its position, and evidently is not in its proper position, even supposing it to represent the Buddha *avatâra* of Vishṇu, which is quite possible. The doorway itself is most elaborately carved, and with its boldly sculptured pillars and pilasters in front, the entrance to the temple forms a very striking and handsome structure.

III. (2) Temple of Râjeśvara. Immediately opposite to the great temple, and only 18 feet distant, stands the small *lingam* temple of Râjeśvara. Its plan is similar to that of the great temple, with a long *maṇḍapa*, open at one end and supported on two rows of pillars down the centre, and a row of pilasters on each side. The *maṇḍapa* is only 22 feet 8 inches long from east to west by 18 feet in breadth. Within is the *linga*.

III. (3) Temple of Râjiva Telin. This is a small building, 5½ feet to the west of the last, now dedicated to Śiva. It is 17 feet 4 inches long by 13 feet broad outside. Inside there is a stone slab, like a common *sati* pillar, with one male figure and three females carved upon it.

III. (4) Temple of Dâneśvara. This is a Śaiva temple of comparatively modern type. It stands immediately to the south of Râjeśvara. It consists of a portico containing a figure of the bull Nandi, and an open *maṇḍapa* of 16 pillars, 25 by 23 feet, with a sanctum $16\frac{1}{2}$ feet square, enshrining the Dâneśvara *linga*.

III. (5) Temple of Jagannâtha. At 15 feet to the east of the Narasinha corner temple, there is a small postern door leading outside to the front of a Vaishṇava temple, dedicated to Vishṇu as Jagannâtha. It is built on the old plan of a *maṇḍapa* closed at the sides, but with the front entirely open. This hall is 28 feet 9 inches long from east to west by 25 feet 5 inches in breadth. Inside is enshrined a wooden figure of Jagannâtha, which is said to have been brought from the great temple in Orissa.

III. (6) Temple of Râmachandra. At a short distance to the south there is a comparatively modern temple said to have been built about 250 years ago (some say 400 years) by Govind Tâl, a Śeth and Bania (banker and grain merchant), who was also the *Kamâdvisdâr* of Râipur. The pillars and pilasters of this temple are all from some older building and are said to have been brought from the ruins at Śirpur. On one of the pilasters there is a short **inscription** of a pilgrim in characters of the 8th or 9th century, reading Śri Lokapâla.

III. (7) Kuleśvara Temple. On an island, which once formed the fork of land between the Pairi and Mahânadi rivers, there is an old temple dedicated to the Kuleśvara *linga*. A stout buttress wall, of an octagonal form, and 16 feet in height, has been built around the temple to preserve it from the encroachments of the two rivers between which it stands. The temple consists of the usual sanctum $14\frac{1}{2}$ feet square outside, with a *maṇḍapa*, or hall leading to it, which is open in front, but closed at the sides like the old temples of the Râjîva-lochana group. A short **inscription** of two lines on one of the pillars records an inundation of former days, which threatened to carry away the temple, a translation of which is "when the waters surrounded the temple of Śiva I stayed here, while Jagal Râv's throne of Śambhu stood firm as a pillar."

The old **inscription** found at Râjim is that of Tivara Deva, who calls himself "King of Kosala." It is engraved on three copper plates, joined by a ring, with a seal attached to it. The seal bears the symbols of Vishṇu, namely, Garuḍa, the lotus, the shell and the discus. The inscription was published in the Asiatic Researches, with a translation by H. H. Wilson, Vol. XV., 508. The plates were found some 5 or 6 feet under ground, close to the temple of Râjîva-lochana. The second and third are those already mentioned as being within the temple of Râjîva-lochana. There are also several records of the visits of pilgrims carved on the pillars of the same temple. (General Cunningham's Reports, Vol. XVII., p. 6.)

III. 31. **Sahâspur** in the Sahâspur-Lohâra *zamindâri*. The remains of a temple with an **inscription** in Sanskrit on the building, which shews that it was built in *Samvat* 924, Kârtika *Sudi* 2nd, by Râṇi Lachmi Devi, who had two sons, Takudeva and Râjadeva, and a daughter, Hasabdevi of Sahâspur. The building is in a dilapidated condition.

III. 32. **Sihawa.** Six old temples, three large and three small, built of stone. Built into the north of the door of one is a slab bearing an **inscription.**

III. 33. **Simgá** is a flourishing old town on the right bank of the Seo, or Seonâth river, 29 miles to the north of Râipur, on the high road to Bilâspur and Ratanpur. The only old monuments are the *sati* pillars, one of which is now in the Ràipur Museum.

III. ✓ 34. **Sirpur,** to the north-east of Râjim and 40 miles lower down the right bank of the Mahânadi river, is the old village which is mentioned as Śripura in a copper plate of the 4th century. The Gandheśvara temple stands on the very brink of the river. The present temple is a comparatively modern one built up of old materials. It is a *lingam* temple. Several sculptures are collected within the enclosure; but the place is chiefly interesting for the inscriptions which have been collected here, as the only temple in Śirpur which is now occupied. There is also an inscription deposited in the Râipur Museum, which is said to have been taken from Śirpur.

There are several temples about half a mile to the north-east of the Gandheśvara temple, one of which, called the Lakshmaṇa temple, is of large size, with the tower in fair preservation. One of the inscription slabs must almost certainly have belonged to this temple. The Lakshmaṇa temple is built on the same plan, and is almost exactly of the same size as the great temple of Râjim. It is built of stone and is still in excellent preservation. The temple itself is of brick and consists of a sanctum and long *maṇḍapa.* The sanctum is still standing with, perhaps, three-fourths of its tower, tolerably perfect; but very little remains of the walls of the *maṇḍapa*, and the pillars and pilasters which once supported the roof are all gone. The carvings on the jambs of the door are of the Gupta style, such as is found at Benâres and Eraṇ. There is a large statue of Vishṇu lying outside the temple which may have belonged to it. The temple seems to have been dedicated to Vishṇu as his *avatâras* are carved on the door jambs, and there is a *varâha* figure on one of the broken pilasters.

There are the remains of two other brick temples close by, of which one is a complete ruin. A portion of the sanctum of the other still remains.

The largest temple at Śirpur is represented by a shapeless mound, now known as the "Surang" or Gallery, from the narrow passages which were found on its excavation. The inscription slab which was found in this temple during its excavation is deposited in the Râipur Museum.

Immediately outside the Gandheśvara temple, on the east, there is a square enclosure surrounded with walls of cut-stone, which the people call the Chhotâ Killâ or "Little Fort," but which seem to be nothing more than the surrounding walls of a great temple. On the west side of the Chhotâ Killâ several sculptures are collected at a place called Devi-ka-sthâna, which derives its name from the principal statue of Mahishâsura-mardani devi, who is represented, as usual, with eight arms killing the buffalo demon. There are numerous broken figures and other remains scattered about the vicinity of the Chhotâ Killâ.

The Rakela Tâl is a fine sheet of water about half a mile to the east of the Gandheśvara temple. It is about 250 or 300 yards square, and to the south there is a ruined fort of about the same dimensions. (General Cunningham's Reports, Vol. VII., p. 168, and Vol. XVII, p. 23.)

III. 35. **Sonábirá,** in the Khairar *zamindâri*. The villagers have set up about eight blocks of stone, each on end, by way of objects of worship; they are from 4 to 6 feet high, and form a miniature Stonehenge; they are daubed with vermillion. The village is far away from all civilisation. (General Cunningham's Reports, Vol. VII., p. 156.)

III. 36. **Sorar,** about eight miles from Bâlod on the road to Dhamtari. Between Sorar and Dhobinpuri, are the remains of a temple known as the house of a Kalâl Râjâ. All now left are two whole and four dwarf pillars with the portions of roof supported by them.

From the village of Navapârâ to Mâjhgâon runs a long stretch of broken blocks of stone lying loose on each other in irregular masses and presenting the exact appearance of the ruins of a great fort two miles long; at intervals stand upright stones looking like *sati* pillars: the whole presents an appearance of great desolation.

Near the ruined temple, cut on a well-smoothed thick slab, is a worn and mutilated *sati* inscription. (Cunningham's Reports, Vol. VII., pp. 137 and 142.)

III. 37. **Titurghát,** in Drug *tehsil*. Temple on the Seonâth river built by the wife of Râjâ Apashal Sing, but not very old.

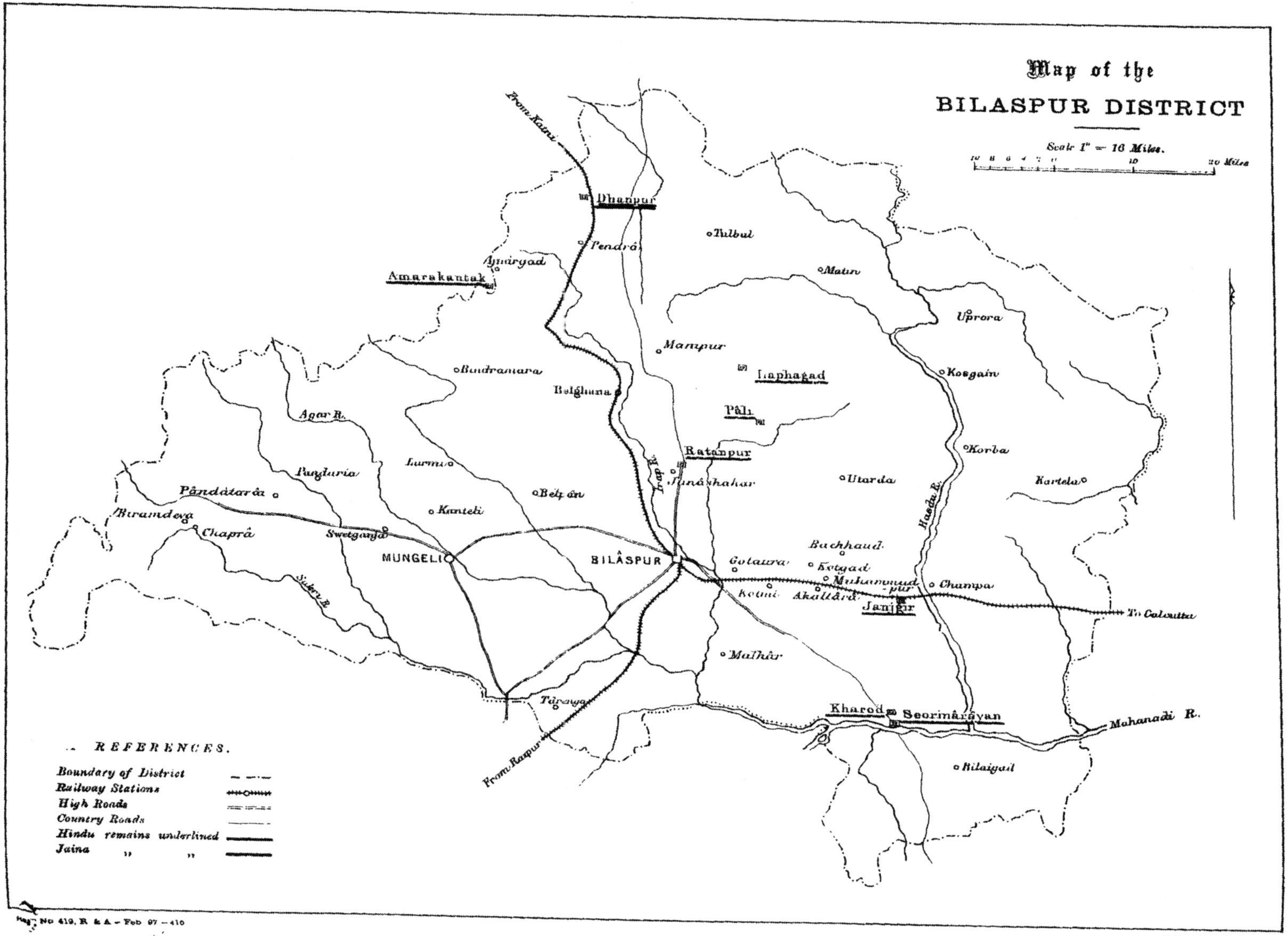
Map of the
BILASPUR DISTRICT
Scale 1" = 16 Miles.
10 8 6 4 2 0 10 20 Miles
From Katni
Dhanpur
Pendrâ
Amargad
Amarakantak
Tulbul
Matin
Uprora
Kosgain
Mampur
Laphagad
Pâli
Budramara
Belghana
Agar R.
Lurmi
Ratanpur
Tuap R.
Junâshahar
Utarda
Korba
Kartela
Hasda R.
Pandaria
Pândâtarâ
Belṭân
Kanteli
Biramdeva
Chaprâ
Swetganga
MUNGELI
BILÂSPUR
Gotawra
Bachhaud
Kotgad
Muhammadpur
Champa
Kotmi
Akaltârâ
Janjgir
To Calcutta
Sukri R.
Malhâr
Târanga
From Raipur
Kharod
Seorinârâyan
Mahanadi R.
Bilaigarh
REFERENCES.
Boundary of District
Railway Stations
High Roads
Country Roads
Hindu remains underlined
Jaina " "
No 419, R & A - Feb 97 - 410
Litho, S I O, Calcutta

II.—Bilâspur.

III. 1. **Bilâspur** contains nothing of note. There are a few statues.

III. 2. **Ajmirgaḍ**, a hill fort about 2 miles to the north of Amarakanṭak. Very little remains of the fort.

III. 3. **Akaltárá**, about 10 miles west of Janjgir, on the route to Bilâspur. Mr. Beglar speaks of "endless fragments of cut and sculptured stone" which were being carted in from the vicinity in (1873-74) and from Kotgaḍ, 3 miles to the north, to build a Bania's house, and in 1875-76 when passing through this place he discovered a fragment of inscription of great interest. There have been at least three old temples here, but only the sites now indicate their former existence.

4. **Amarakantak** in the hills in the north of Bilâspur, is the source of the Narmadâ and Son rivers. It forms the extreme eastern peak of the Mahikâl range of hills. It is a great place for pilgrims, some on their way to or from Jagannâtha from Upper India, others doing the *pradakshiṇâ* of the Narmadâ. The objects of veneration at Amarakanṭak are the statues of Narmadâ Mâi, the various *Śaiva-lingas* and statues, and some Vaishṇava ones, while the holy *kuṇḍa* at the head of the infant river is considered all-powerful in washing away sins.

IIb. (1). Architecturally, however, there is but one temple of interest, and that is the great deserted one known as the Karṇa Mandira and traditionally ascribed to Karṇa Râjâ. As it stands at present, it has the appearance of three distinct temples on one large raised platform, but this is due either to the great connecting *mahâmaṇḍapa* having been destroyed or never completed, and it was no doubt intended as a three-shrined temple. The mouldings are bold and elegant but perfectly plain, as is in fact the whole temple; the little carving that exists is confined to the upper portions of the towers, and is merely of the plain horse-shoe type. This is the oldest existing temple in the place; it is neglected, but a few pilgrims visit it and place offerings of flowers on the Śaivic emblems.

III. (2). Two hundred feet to the north of this is a half-ruined temple, consisting simply of a cell with a portico, the latter being supported upon fourteen pillars and two pilasters. The spire has fallen in. The temple seems to be much more recent than the great Karṇa temple, and both material and execution are coarse.

III. (3), (4) and (5). To the north of the last are three small temples in a line which consist of only a cell each with a small tower roof.

III. (6). To the west of these is a large temple facing north, ascribed to the Bhonsles; it is well plastered over but not whitewashed; to the west of this is another similar one facing east; the two are joined together, forming a single temple by being made to open into a common *maṇḍapa*, whose entrance faces east; Gaṇeśa is over the doorway at the east end. In the west sanctum is a four-armed statue, as also in the south one. The statues are fine ones.

III. (7). To the north of this is another large temple. The hall is open all round to within a couple of feet of the floor, and is supported upon sixteen pillars, pilasters, and dwarf pillars. The temple faces east and has Gaṇeśa sculptured over the doorway.

III. (8). To the east of this is a small half ruined temple, consisting of only a cell and an *antarâla*; the *maṇḍapa* has, probably, disappeared long ago. This temple, judging from the execution, style and weathering, appears to be old. It faces north. The sanctum contains a four-armed female statue said to represent Narmadâ Mâi, but she has now only three arms left, the fourth having been broken off.

III. (9). Almost touching this temple, and to the east, is another temple quite ruined, leaving the back wall and portions of side walls of the sanctum alone standing. The temple is similar in appearance, material, and execution to the last described. It faces east and enshrines a four-armed male statue fully equal to the four-armed female statue in the last temple in excellence. The statue is now known as the statue of the Son river god, but it is undeniably one of Vishṇu, holding in the four hands the *śankha*, *chakra*, *gadâ*, and lotus, and the fish and tortoise are sculptured on either side of the head. Altogether this statue is a very fine specimen of sculpture. These two temples are the only ones that can be ascribed to an age rivalling, if not surpassing, that of the Karṇa temple, but both are much ruined.

III. (10). To the east of this is a large temple of Mahâdeva similar to temple No. (7).

III. (11). To the north of No. (8) is a small modern shrine.

III. (12). To the north-west of this is a group of recently erected temples consisting of a central *chhatri* with two pairs of *charaṇas*, or foot-prints, sculptured on stone in the centre. The surrounding temples are four in number containing statues of Hunamân, Gaṇeśa, a coarsely executed seated figure of Śiva, and a four-armed one of Vishṇu, the last a fine statue and probably taken from some older temple.

III. (13). To the west of this is a small modern shrine.

III. (14). At the north-east corner of No. (12) group is a small temple, facing north, of Mahâdeva, with horse-shoe arched doorways.

III. Near the north end of this group of temples are the remains of a reservoir with *pakka* sides, which must once have been the holy *kuṇḍa* of Narmadâ. It is now nearly full of earth, but there is still a little water in its hollows. It is entirely disused. Beyond this reservoir are the recent groups of temples, beginning with a solitary stuccoed small modern temple. To the north-west of this, about 200 feet distant, a similar one, and another 200 feet, to the north-east of this one, is a large temple facing east, and close to it another similar one. To the north of these is the present holy *kuṇḍa*, or reservoir, with flights of steps and masonry revetments. This *kuṇḍa*, as may be expected, is full of particularly dirty water, loaded as it is with the moral and physical filth from numberless pilgrims. A small trickling stream issues from a hole in the west wall of the reservoir and runs westward. This is the Narmadâ which, two miles further, falls over the descent of seventy feet in what is known as the Kapila Dhârâ. In the reservoir are three temples or *chhatris*, all small and recent. To the west of the reservoir are two temples, quite modern; while upon the northern bank are three small old-looking half ruined temples. Close to these is a small *chabutrâ* with a *linga* on top, and to the east of the *chabutrâ* is a modern small temple facing east. Among the miscellaneous fragments on this side is a much worn **inscription** in a half ruined small temple, a fine statue, three feet high, of an elephant, and a fragment of a horse two feet high. The other **inscriptions**, besides the one on the steps, on the *chabutrâ*, and the broken slab, are—one on a statue known as the Revâ Nâyaka statue in the *chhatri* in the tank; one on a similar statue in a small temple much worn, merely a record of a worshipper; and an **inscription** in three and a half lines on a similar statue, in one of the small temples dated *Samvat* 922.

III. At the head of the roadway stands the great double temple of Narmadâ Mài. This temple consists of two sanctums opposite each other, facing east and west and opening into a common pillared hall. Behind these are two small temples, half ruined. Behind, and to the north of this group, flows the Sâvitri *nâlâ*, which is the real source of the Narmadâ, as, where it joins the rivulet issuing from the *kuṇḍa* it is both larger and carries down a greater volume of water. It also drains a greater basin above the junction than the rivulet issuing from the *kuṇḍa* does. (General Cunningham's Reports, Vol. VII., p. 227.)

III. 5. **Bachhaud,** 5 miles to the west of Bâludâ, and about 14 miles north-west of Janjgir. Here is a fort, said to be of stone and brick with an arched gateway still in existence.

III. 6. **Belpán,** a temple which enjoys the revenues of the village.

III. 7. **Bilaigaḍ,** a chiefship in the Bilâspur district. Here are the remains of an extensive fort and the ruins of some ancient temples.

IIb. 8. **Biramdeva,** 10 miles north of Kâwardhâ in the Feudatory State of the same name. This temple is one of the most ancient in the district, it is said to date from A.D. 103 (?). The **inscription** sets forth that one of the Hai Hai Bansi Râjâs of Ratanpur tried to prevent its construction, but was repulsed.

9. **Chaprá** probably the same as Biramdeva.

10. **Chhattisgaḍ** or Mahâ-Kosala. Mahâ-Kosala comprised the whole of the upper valley of the Mahânadi and its tributaries, from the source of the Narmadâ at Amarakanṭak, on the north, to the source of the Mahânadi itself, near Kânkar, on the south, and from the valley of the Wen Gangâ on the west, to the Hàrdâ and Jonk rivers on the east. But these limits have often been extended, so as to embrace the hilly districts of Mandlâ and Bâlâghât on the west up to the banks of the

Wen Gangâ, and the middle valley of the Mahânadî, on the east, down to Sambalpur and Sonpur. Its name of Chhattisgaḍ means the country of the "thirty-six forts." For a full account of this district see General Cunningham's Report, XVII., page 68, and also Vol. VII., p. 224.

III. 11. **Dhanpur,** about 5 miles to the north of Pendrâ. Here are the ruins of Dhanpur, from whence numerous statues, stones, and ancient fragments are being, and have long been brought to Pendrâ, which is the head-quarters of the Pendrâ chief. The ruins are very extensive, covering nearly four square miles of ground; the great mass of the ruins are, however, compressed within an area of barely half a square mile. Amongst these is the great tank known as the Bhantara tank; here are several fragments of sculpture. Half a mile to the north of the tank are several low mounds scattered about in scrub jungle; the first group consists of six temples; half a mile to the west of this is a group of ruins of four temples,
III. besides several smaller detached or isolated shrines close by. To the north of these is a long chain of tanks. Upon the low rugged hillocks on the opposite bank of the tanks is a mound of ruins consisting of a group of four large temples apparently Jaina. Not far from these is the tank known as Sobhanâtha, on the margin of which are collected numerous Jaina fragments. Among the ruins Brahmanical statues are to be seen; the tank close to the ruins of the first group is called Katha *talâv.* The temples are of brick and stone, and also exclusively of stone, the bricks being of the very large old pattern such as found at Śirpur. The ruins might repay further exploration as much may be hidden away in the jungle around. (Cunningham's Reports, Vol. VII., page 237.)

II*b*. 12. **Gotaura,** 8 miles west-north-west of Kotmi. Here are numerous statues carefully executed and finished in black stone, and in excellent preservation. There are the sites of several temples.

II*b*. 13. **Janjgir,** about 22 miles north of Seorinârâyan. Here are two temples, one of which is much dilapidated, and the other never was finished. These are the only two existing temples, but there is no doubt that others also existed in ancient times. Architecturally the temples are very interesting. The smaller of the two is complete and is profusely sculptured; it would seem to have been Vaishṇava. There are on the temple in two spaces between the sculptured scenes two mutilated lines of **inscription.** For a full description of these temples and statues see Cunningham's Reports, Vol VII., p. 204 *et seq.* Sixteen miles due north of Janjgir and 8 miles to the north-east of Bâludâ is said to be a cave in the hills containing fine sculptures, pillars, etc.

II*b*. 14. **Junâshahar** close to Ratanpur. Here are the remains of several buildings, and on the hills are a few temples, but there is nothing of great antiquity or even of interest.

III. 15. **Kharod,** 3 miles to the north-west of Seorinârâyan. The temple of Lakshmeśvara, though not the oldest, is certainly the largest and most important

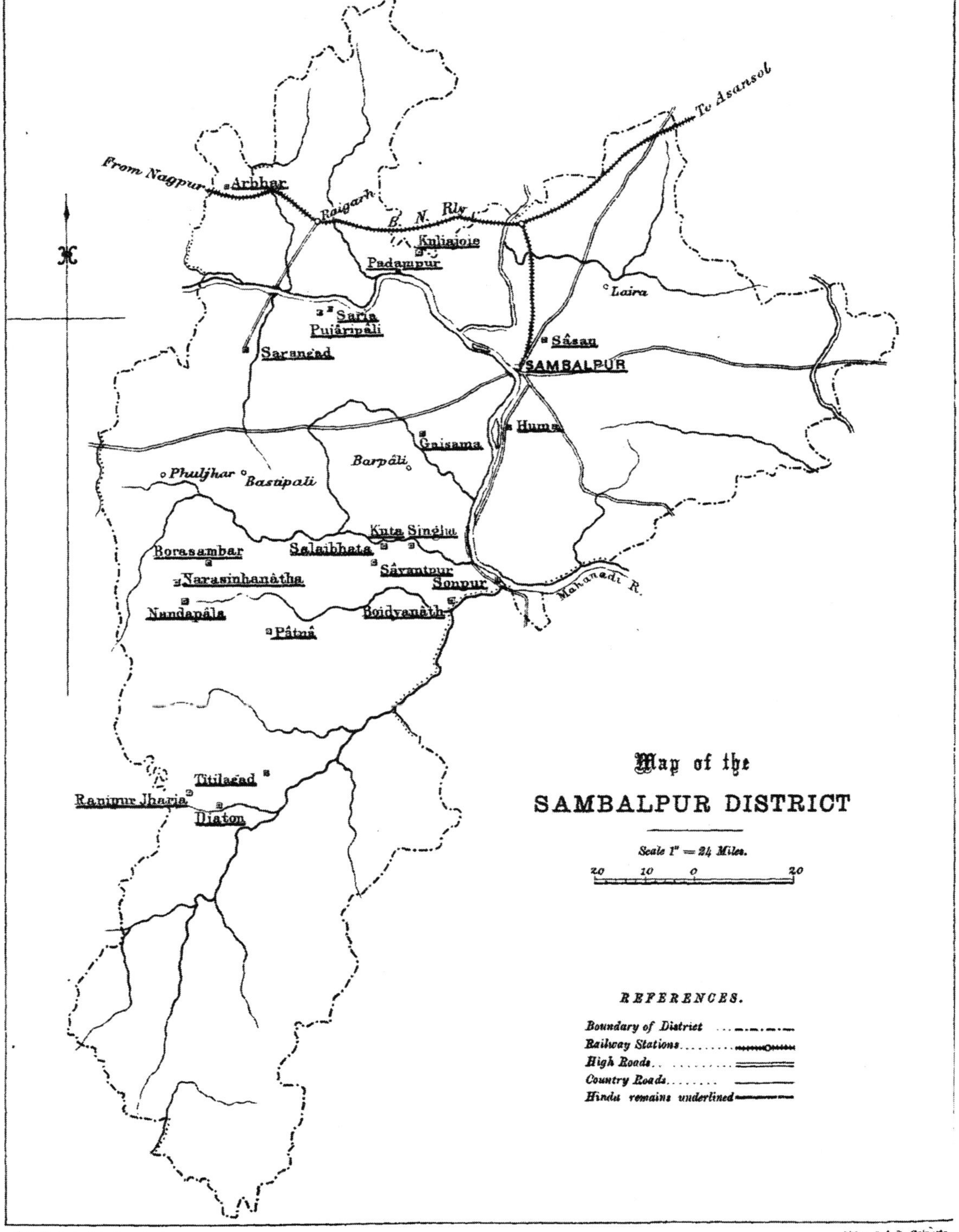

Reg No 419 I. & A.—Misc. 97.—410 Litho., S. I. O., Calcutta.

III.—Sambalpur.

III. 1. **Sambalpur.** Here there is a fort situated to the north-west of the town proper; nothing remains of it but the crumbling stone wall on the river face, and a few mouldering bastions. The remains of the moat are still visible, but it has been here and there filled up. The only gateway left is that of Samlâi near the temple of the goddess Samlâi, who was apparently the tutelar deity of Sambalpur. There are several other temples also within the precincts, the principal of which are those of Padmeśvarî Devî, Barâ Jagannâtha, and Ananta Sajjâ, all built between the year 1500 and 1600 A.D. They are of uniform design, and neither remarkable for beauty of architecture nor for solidity of structure. There are also some remains of dwellings of former râjâs within the fort, but most of them were in such a dilapidated condition as to make their removal necessary. One only, which has some little pretensions to appearance, was to have been repaired and made available for the accommodation of the Native Chief visiting Sambalpur. (See also General Cunningham's Reports, XVII., 59.)

IIb. 2. **Arbhar**, about 85 miles north-west of Sambalpur. Here there are some remains of an old temple constructed of fine brown stone without mortar, and is decorated with sculpture. It measures 25 yards by 16 yards. The temple was dedicated to Kâlî, whose image still exists in the middle of the building. It has fallen, and the only remains which now exist are two doorways, one before and the other behind the image. There are some inscriptions in *Devanâgari* characters.

III. 3. **Barpâli**, 34 miles south-west of Sambalpur. Temple of Somleśvarî, said to be 500 years old, which was built by Bikram Singh, one of the ancestors of the present *Zamindâr* of the place. Also the temple of Jagannâtha, supposed to have been built 490 years ago by Hirday Sâi, also one of the *Zamindârs* of the place.

III. 4. **Bastipâli**, 10 miles east of Sarâipâli. An old temple and a fort, but of no particular interest.

III. 5. **Borasambar**, 8 miles south-west from Padampur. An old temple, constructed of rough stones and mortar, dedicated to Patmâheśvarî. The image was established here by a former *Zamindâr* of Borasambar.

III 6. **Gaisama**, 25 miles south-west of Sambalpur. The temple of Bâlukeśvara. Râjâ Abboy Singh had gone to visit the temple, and the priest requested the Râjâ to accept the offerings of the god. The king observed a hair in the flower given to him and was somewhat puzzled; but the clever priest explained that the deity had hairs on his head like a man. The Râjâ ordered a *pakka* temple to be constructed in honour of the god, who had hair like a man.

III. 7. **Gaḍ Phuljhar,** 14 miles south of Sarâipâli. A temple with a fort around is alleged to have been constructed by Râjâ Anant Sâi of Phuljhar, about 200 years ago. Near it is situated a tank called Mânasarobara. Is in the possession of the Râṇi of Phuljhar and is somewhat out of repairs.

III. 8. **Huma,** 14 miles south of Sambalpur. Temple of Mahâdeva. This temple was built in the reign of Balair Singh Mahârâja. The worship of Mahâdeva is said to have been begun by a Gour who daily crossed the Mahânadî to a place where the underlying rock cropped out on the bank. Here he daily offered his dole of milk, which was at once drunk up by the rock. The strangeness of this event led to enquiries which ended in the construction of the present temple.

It is a noted place for pilgrimage; and an annual fair is held here and is visited by strangers out of curiosity to see the different kinds of fish, which are so tame that they eat sweetmeats from the hands of those who bathe in the Mahânadî stream close to the temple.

9. **Jhária,** *see* Râṇipur Jhârial.

III. 10. **Kuliajoie** in Korabaga, 31 miles north-west of Sambalpur. The temple of Maheśvara Bâbâ. This is supposed to be of superhuman construction. It is a place of pilgrimage. There is a water-fall near the temple and the pool at the foot of the fall abounds in fish and snakes. The deity Maheśvara is said to dwell in this pool. There is a cave in the adjoining rocks said to be the resting place of the Bhau. It is called Maheśvaranâtha.

III. 11. **Láira,** 28 miles north-east of Sambalpur. A broken temple. Tradition has it that some 200 years ago one Jewar Gond had a dream which acquainted him with the secret that there was a temple under the ground where he lay. With difficulty he induced the people to believe him; but on the place being dug up the dream was shown to be true.

III. 12. **Narasinhanâtha,** 20 miles west of Padampur. An old temple constructed of rough stone and mortar and plastered, dedicated to Narasinhanâtha. It is a place of importance to pilgrims, and is in the possession of the *Zamindār* of Borasambar. The income derived from the pilgrims is devoted to the use of the temple. There is a large annual fair. The temple has two sculptured stone doorways. It is being repaired by the Court of Wards. There is an **inscription** in five lines in Oriya characters.

III. 13. **Padampur,** 36 miles north-west of Sambalpur. The temple of Padmâsani supposed to have been built by the descendants of the Ganga dynasty in *Samvat* 1510 during the reign of Bahâr Singh Deva, Maharâjâ of Sambalpur. Also the Gopinâtha and Jagannâtha Mandira said to have been built by the same king.

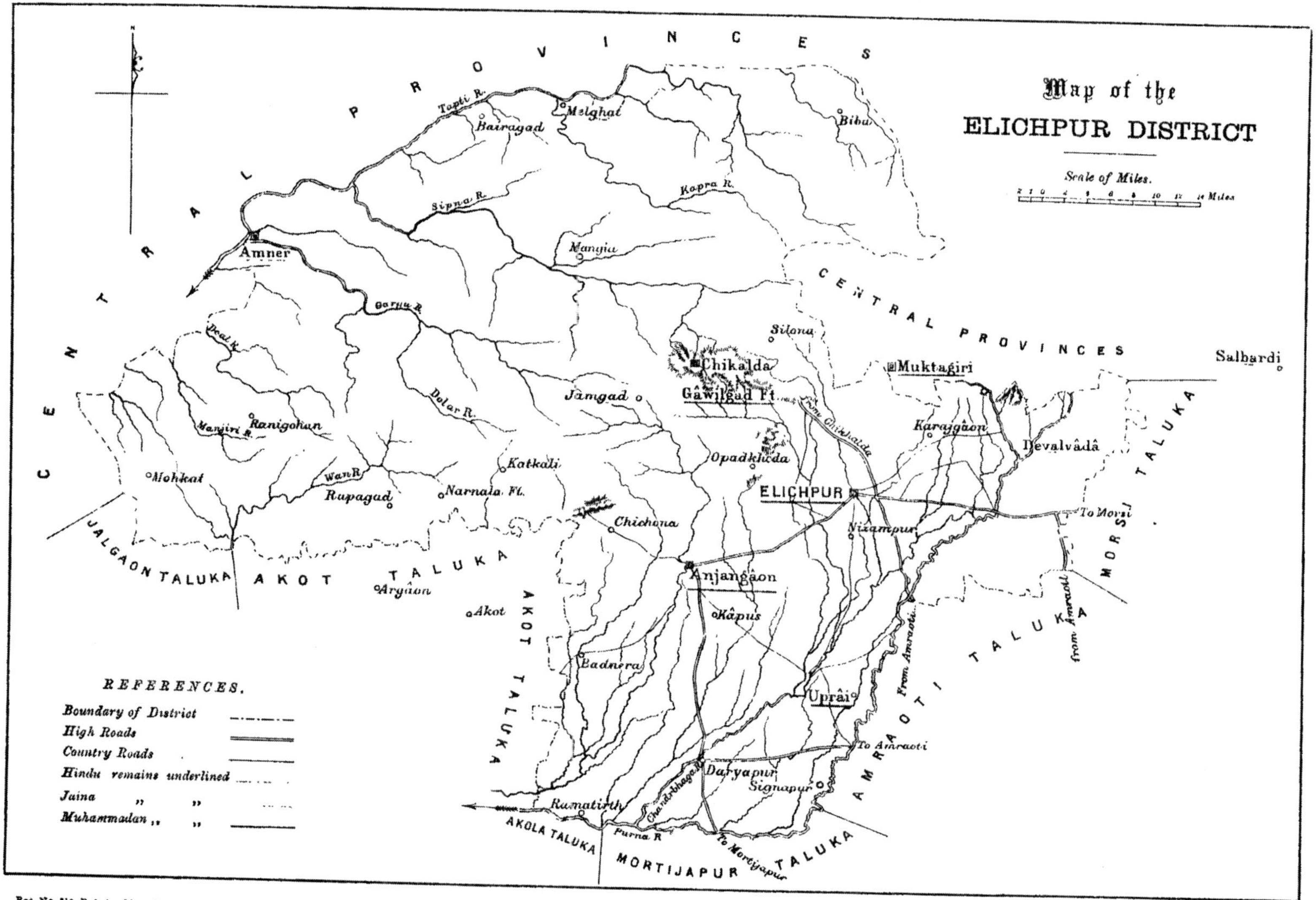

Reg No 510, R. & A.—Ma: 96.—410

Litho, S. I. O., Calcutta

temple of Mahâdeva, on the bank of a *nâlâ*, surrounded by hills. It is in good repair.

III 31. **Jambhora,** 4 miles to the south of Chikhli. An old temple of Mahâdeva. It is in good repair.

III. 32. **Jogdari,** 10 miles west of Mehkar. An old temple of Mahâdeva, of good workmanship. Has a very good image in the shrine.

III. 33. **Kalambeśvara,** 12 miles north of Mehkar. An old step-well with four flights of steps on four sides, and a small shrine of Devî in its southern side. It is in good repair.

III. 34. **Karvand,** 8 miles north-east of Chikhli. A small old temple of Mahâdeva which stands to the south of the village. It is in good repair.

III. 35. **Kinhola,** 6 miles north of Chikhli. An old temple of Mahâdeva.

III. 36. **Kothali.** An old temple of Chintâmaṇi Mahâdeva, but of no interest.

III. 37. **Linga,** 9 miles west of Mehkar. An old temple of Mahâdeva which stands to the west of the village and not far from it. It is in good repair.

38. **Lonár,** nearly 12 miles south of Mehkar. Several Hemâdpanti temples and tanks, also a Hindu temple which has evidently been originally a Hemâdpanti, if not Buddhist structure. Below this temple is a tank with flights of steps and terraces leading down to it. The water flows through the sculptured image of a bullock, and is fabled to come underground all the way from the Ganges. It is curious as there is no apparent watershed. People of all except low castes—men, women and children—bathe promiscuously in it. The water is constantly changed as it passes through one aperture at the bottom as fast as it flows in. Low castes use the dirty water as it passes out below. Below the Hindu temple is the salt lake leading down to which there has been a magnificent flight of steps, a large portion of which still remains.

Regarding this salt lake there is a wonderful legend of a giant named Lonâsura who lived in a subterraneous abode, made by himself, under a hill, about a mile from the place where the village of Lonâr now stands. When this monster had destroyed many human beings and animals, and threatened to overthrow even the gods, the latter became alarmed and supplicated Vishṇu to relieve them from the danger. Vishṇu assumed the form of a beautiful youth to gain over the assistance of the gaint's two sisters. By their assistance he discovered the subterraneous dwelling, and with a touch of his toe he threw off the covering of the den and found the giant asleep. Engaging in single combat with him Vishṇu slew him, and buried him in the very pit he had made his home: this was the present salt lake of Lonâr. Its water is supposed to be his blood, and the salt is his decomposed flesh. A hill standing, according to the Berâr Gazetteer, 36 miles to the south-west of Lonâr, but according to an informant only about a koss from it (?), is said to be the lid of the den thrown off by Vishṇu, and is reported to coincide in shape and size with the surface of the lake.

The lake is about a mile across, or three miles round, and is supposed to be the crater of an ancient volcano. Round the top of the basin is about five miles, and the sides slope abruptly down, and are covered with jungle and trees extending in parts to the margin of the lake in which panthers and wild hog are occasionally found, and in which pea-fowl generally abound. Nearly in the centre of the lake are said to be two deep fissures hitherto unfathomed, through which impregnation takes place during the monsoon, when only pure crystals of salt are obtained from their edges by divers. But to enter these openings during the hot season would be certain death. Evaporation takes place to a very considerable extent during the hot season, and leaves a crystallized deposit upon the surface that gives the lake the appearance of being frozen over. This deposit is carefully collected as the water evaporates, as well as the earth beneath it, which is also to a certain extent impregnated. These deposits were formerly very valuable, and yielded a handsome revenue to Government. The rent at present is Rupees 4,000 per annum for a five years' lease, and this is regarded by the contractors as unprofitable as the lake has not dried up for many years.

Ib. (1) The finest temple is within the village to the south within a mud wall. Forty years ago the whole basement was buried in debris, but the sculptures were far more perfect than they are now. The basement has been unearthed, and the temple otherwise thrown open, and now the first sight of it takes one by surprise.

It is built on a basement of very considerable extent and varying in height from five feet four inches to eight feet. The general form of this basement is that of a cross measuring from east to west about 106 feet, and from north to south 84 feet. The corners are broken up in the usual manner by a number of re-entrant angles. On the east face a flight of steps (seven) ten feet eight inches wide leads on to the terrace which is seventeen feet broad by sixteen feet three inches in depth. Here is the principal entrance to the temple by a door eight feet four inches high by three feet eight inches wide. On the north side the corresponding seven steps are seven feet nine inches by three feet six inches, while on the south side there are eight steps eight feet five inches wide, and a door seven feet three inches by three feet four inches. The whole of the interior or nearly so has fallen in and is supported by about two-and-twenty arches of brick and mortar. The *maṇḍapa* has been twenty-eight feet four inches by twenty-eight feet seven inches, supported by four columns enclosing a slightly raised platform. These columns measure three feet five inches at the base, and, so far as can be estimated, have been about ten feet high. Opposite each pillar has been a pilaster with demi-pilasters in the corners and midway between these on each wall an additional pilaster, except on the right side of the north door, where there is a niche apparently opening into a reservoir of water. No remains of the ceiling or dome now exist. The anti-chamber is eleven feet two inches broad by ten feet deep; the doorway has gone and has been built up with brick and mortar; pilasters and semi-pilasters support one architrave two feet nine inches thick, over which is an octagonal frieze apparently sculptured with troops. The angles below

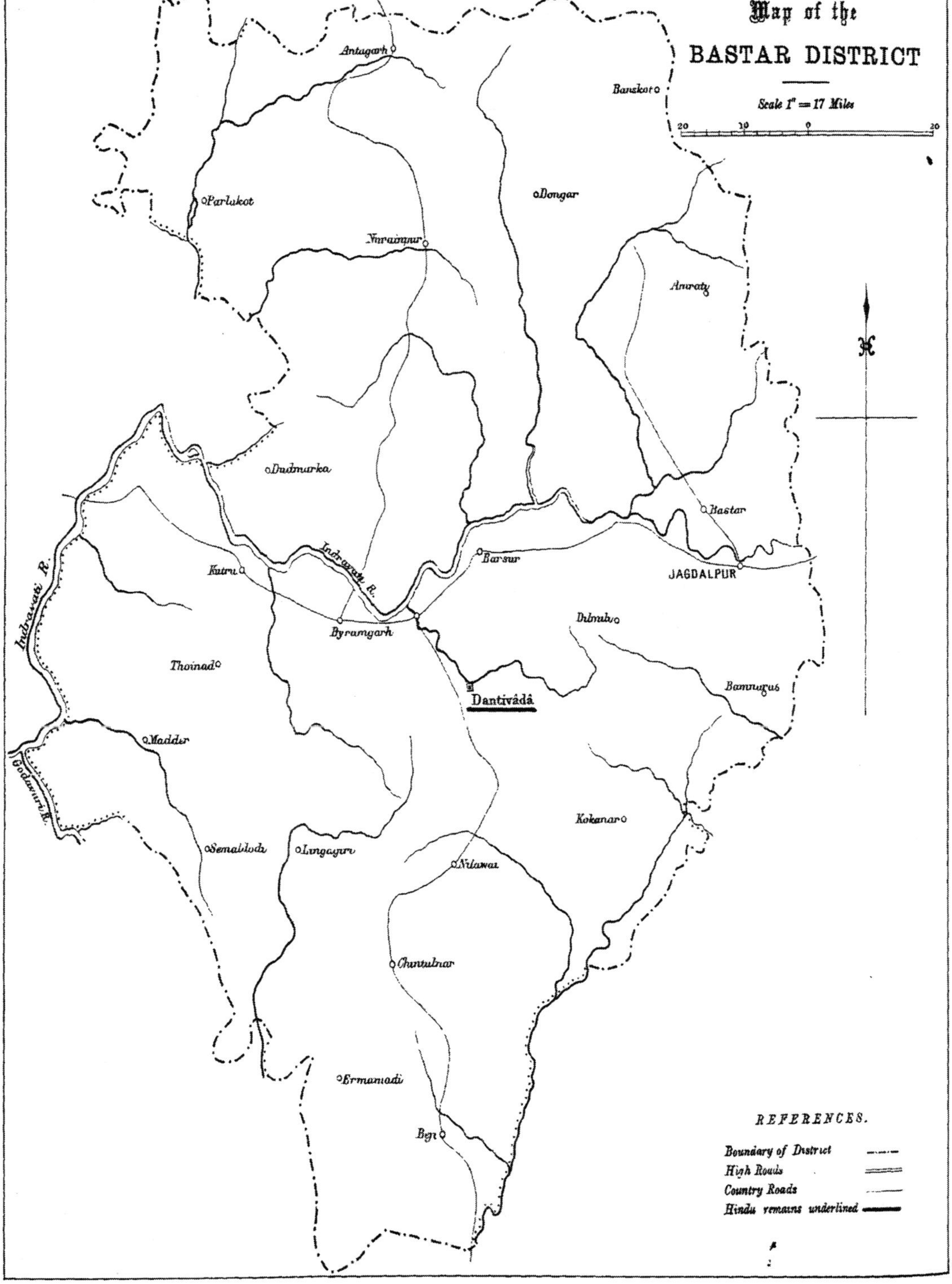

Reg No 419, R & A—Feb. 97—410

Litho S I O, Calcutta

III. 14. **Phuljhar,** *see* Gaḍ Phuljhar.

IIb. 15. **Pujâripâli** in Sârangaḍ. Two old temples standing, and the remains of what is said to have been the Râṇi's Palace. Both the temples are of brick, with stone casings carved in the usual ancient fashion. One of the temples has a Sanskṛit **inscription** of considerable length. Both the temples appear to have been dedicated originally to Mahâdeva, but in one of them some hideous wooden idols from Jagannâtha have now been placed. It is stated that 120 temples once stood in and about Pujâripâli. (Cunningham's Reports, XVII., 68.)

IIb. 16. **Saria,** or Pujaripâli. Here are two old temples dedicated to Śiva and Jagannâtha respectively. One of the buildings is said to be the palace of the Râṇi. They are built of brick and of stones with carvings thereon. *See* Pujâripâli.

III. 17. **Sâsan,** 8 miles north of Sambalpur, the Gopinâtha Mandira was built in Ajit Singh's reign, but being in a dilapidated condition it was subsequently repaired by Hari Guru with the aid of collections raised from Brâhmaṇas.

Feudatory States under the Chhattishgaḍ Political Agency.

IIb. 1. **Boidyanâth** in Sonpur. The temple of Kuśaleśvarî. There is a tradition that this temple was built by Anang Bhîma Gajpati, Râjâ of Orissa, in bygone ages with the help of the masons imported from Northern India. There are **inscriptions** on some of the stones on the top of the temple. They cannot be properly deciphered. The skill and art displayed in the construction of this temple are admirable. Also the temple of Kâleśvara, which was built during the reign of Anang Bhîma Deva at about the same time as the first temple.

III. 2. **Diaton** in the Pâtnâ State. Śaiva temple called "Brâhmaṇi Gudi."

III. 3. **Kuta Singha** in Pâtnâ State. Birinchi Nârâyaṇa Gudi. This is an old temple built of large blocks of sandstone obtained from the neighbouring village. The legend is that it was erected by two women, sisters-in-law, who also had a tank dug close by. There was an image of the sun called Birinchi Nârâyaṇa, but it has long since disappeared.

III. 4. **Nandapâla** in Pàtnâ State. The temple of Hari-Śaṅkara. In ancient days there lived two brothers called Hari and Sahadeva of Sipka, Khonds by caste. Jamunâ was the name of the wife of Hari, and Rodnâ that of Sahadeva. Jamunâ once went to the mountain of Gandha Mâdan in search of roots. While digging up a root called *pita kanda*, she observed a white milky juice issuing forth from it; and immediately afterwards she heard a sound like the mewing of a cat, and perceived beneath her spade a stone image shaped like a cat. Then a voice said distinctly:—Know that the deity Narasinha dwells here and he does not deserve to be so contemptuously treated as to suffer the strokes of thy spade. Jamunâ took fright at this occurrence and fled from the spot. Next day she returned, accompanied by her husband Hari. The god Narasinha, being propitiated, was much pleased, and directed Hari to remove him from that place and commence worshipping him. Hari accordingly took the stone image in the shape of a cat and returned home. This happened during the reign of Harinâtha, king of Jhâria and Râmpûr. Jamunâ went to the king and related the whole occurrence to him. The Râjâ was astonished and in commemoration of the event installed the image in a temple in the village of Harranpap, in the Borasambar State. After this it was revealed to Harinâtha's queen in a dream that the gods Mahâdeva and Lakshmaṇa Deva would manifest themselves at the village of Nandapâla. When the queen visited the village she found two stone images of the gods. She built them a shrine.

An **inscription** occurs on the door frame. At present the temple is occupied by Mahâdeva. On the southern side of the hill is a temple called *Deval Durla*, after the name of the Râṇi who constructed it. Close to the temple is a thatched hut in which the image of Bhairava is enshrined. On this, too, there is an **inscription** in old characters. Not very far off is a cave, excavated in the side of the hill, within which are placed five colossal images representing the five Pâṇḍavas, who are said to have spent a portion of their long period of banishment in this sequestered spot. This is a famous place of pilgrimage. (Cunningham's Reports, XVII., 65.)

III. 5. **Pátná,** chief town of the Pâtnâ State. Pâtnâ appears to be the most ancient principality in the district. Long before the establishment of Sambalpur, Pâtnâ already possessed temples and other buildings of artistic interest, as is evident from the fact that Balrâma Deva, a member of the Pâtnâ Royal family, founded the Sambalpur town, and introduced into it the religious institutions already established at Pâtnâ. Thus we find in Sambalpur the temple of the goddess Samlâi, the Brahmapura temple, and the temple of Kuśaleśvara, all of which are imitations of similar religious buildings at Pâtnâ.

The temple of Kuśaleśvara is situated not very far from the Pâtnâ Râjâ's house. The old temple was broken down by Râjâ Bajra Hiradhor Deva, who built the present temple dedicated to Kuśaleśvara. In the old temple of Pâtneśvara, an image of Durgâ with ten arms was enshrined. In front of the temple there is a small shrine dedicated to Champâ Telini. In front of the temple there are some square stone pillars. It is said that the ceremony of coronation of the Pâtnâ Râjâs was performed here. There is an **inscription** in ancient characters on one of the pillars. (Cunningham's Reports, XVII., 63.)

In the Original Lists there is the following note of a temple of Siddheśvara.—When the foundation of the temple was being excavated some stone pillars were found with *Devanâgari* characters inscribed on them; also a box with bones and heads. From the **inscription** it appears that the original temple must have been erected in 1252. A queen had offered herself *sati* and in her memory the pillars were constructed.

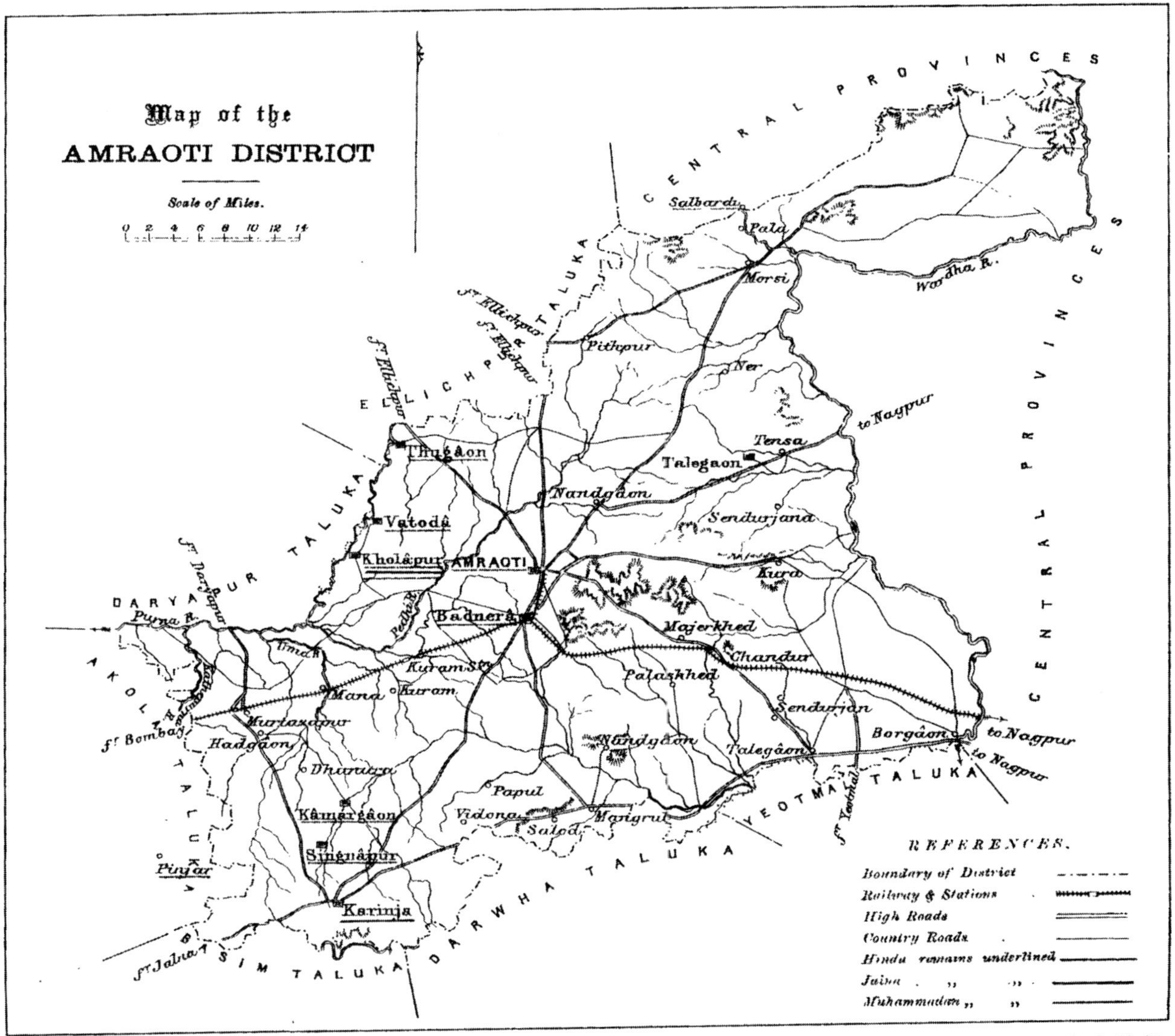

Ref. No 610 R. & A.—Mar. 06 110

Litho., S. I. O. Calcutta.

II.—Elichpur.

III. 1. **Elichpur** a well-known capital during the middle ages. Little now remains of the period anterior to 1720, excepting a building called the "Hauz Katorah," and a channel conveying the water of the Bichan, which runs through the present cantonments to the city. The principal places of interest are—Dulla Rahimân's Dargâh, the ruins of the palace built by Salâbat Khân and Ismâel Khân, the tombs of the Navâbs, Fazlu Miyan's tombs, and a few others, but none of any particular interest from an archæological point of view.

III. 2. **Ámner**, 32 miles north-west of Elichpur, situated at the junction of the Garga and Tâpti rivers. There is an old temple to Mahâdeva, on the banks of the river, and, about 30 paces off, a pool, the depth of which is unknown; at the bottom there is said to be a temple which can be seen when the river is clear. Also a fort, often called Jilpi Âmner. It occupies an elevated position at the junction of the Garga and Tâpti. It is a compact looking quadrangular building of brick and mud pointed with mortar. The walls are flanked by four round bastions of the same material, and enclose about an acre of ground. The west angle is occupied by a mosque, which, with its minarets towering above the rest of the fort, presents rather a picturesque object. There is only one approach, that from the north-west, on a level with the left bank of the Tâpti which, though here entirely of earth, is very steep and lofty. The gateway and a portion of the ramparts were destroyed in 1858. At the same time the guns, four or five in number, were removed.

III. 3. **Anjangáon**, 14 miles south-west from Elichpur. Temples of Mahâdeva and Viṭhobâ, and a mosque, all of the 18th century; a *haveli* or palace of the 17th.

4. **Chikaldá**, *see* Gawilgaḍ.

III. 5. **Devalvádá**, a village on the Pûrnâ, about 14 miles from Elichpur. According to Hindu mythology, this is the place where Narasinha, after killing Hîraṇya Kaśipu, was able, after failing everywhere else, to wash the blood-stains from his hands. There is a temple and idol to Narasinha, which has been here from time immemorial, with steps to the river, and a *ghât*. There is also a temple to "Viṭthala Rukhmâi" built in the time of Salâbat Khân by one Mahâdev Râv Lakshmaṇ of Nâgpur, at a cost of ₨15,000; also a *masjid* built some three hundred years ago.

III. 6. **Gáwilgaḍ** fort, close to Chikaldâ, and about 14 miles north-west of Elichpur. It is "situated on a range of mountains between the sources of the rivers Pûrnâ and Tâpti. It stands on a lofty mountain in this range, and consists of one complete inner fort which fronts to the south, where the rock is most steep, and an outer fort which covers the inner to the north and north-west. This outer fort has a third wall, which covers the approach to it from the north by the village of Labâda. All these walls are strongly built and fortified by ramparts and towers. The communications with the fort are through three gates—one to the south with the inner fort, one to the north-west with the outer fort, and one to the north with the third wall."*

III. 7. **Manjira** in the Melghât. Nearly opposite to the village, on the western face of a hill to the west of the valley, are two small rock-cut temples or monasteries. One is completely closed up with rubbish, but a short flight of steps leads down from the platform in front to the entrance of the other by a low doorway. This cave is about 16 feet square inside, and not more than 7 or 8 feet high; there are two rows of square pillars extending inwards. They are quite plain, being rather roughly hewn, and there is no attempt at any curious carving about any of them. The interior ones are left half finished, the excavator having evidently met with some interruption which prevented the completion of his design. The platform of the caves is some 50 feet below the upper surface of the hill, from which it is reached by rather a difficult scramble over some large boulders, where no one would think of going without some special object.

On the plateau, not far from these caves, is a spring of most delicious water which is never dry. A basin about 5 feet square and 6 feet deep has been cut in the rock, which is here close to the surface to receive the water. At the bottom the basin is under-cut, rude pillars of natural rock having been left to support the superincumbent mass. A second and third excavation of a similar kind occur in a line with the first, but the former are now choked up. This was, no doubt, intended for the supply of water to the monastery for which the caves just described were most probably designed.

8. **Muktagiri** in the Betul district and just across the border, about 13 miles north-east of Elichpur. (See Central Provinces' List.)

9. **Sálburdi,** just across the border, about 32 miles north-east of Elichpur, in the Betul district. (See Central Provinces' List.)

10. **Singnápur,** in the Daryâpur *tâlukâ*, 14 miles south-east of Daryâpur. A brick temple of Hanumân, perhaps of the early part of the 16th century.

III. 11. **Uprái,** a small village in Daryâpûr *tâlukâ,* on the banks of the Pûrnâ, about 18 miles due south of Elichpur. A celebrated tomb, called Shâh Dâwal, being in memory of a Musalmân named Shâh and a Mahâr named Dâwal, who came together from Hindusthân some two hundred years ago, settled in the village, and on dying were buried in one tomb. Both Hindus and Muhammadans worship here and it is the custom to pray before the shrine previous to any work being undertaken or when any gift is particularly desired. A fair is held here once a year.

* Colonel Wellesley's despatch after the fall of the fort in 1803, also Berâr Gazetteer, 1870, p. 143.

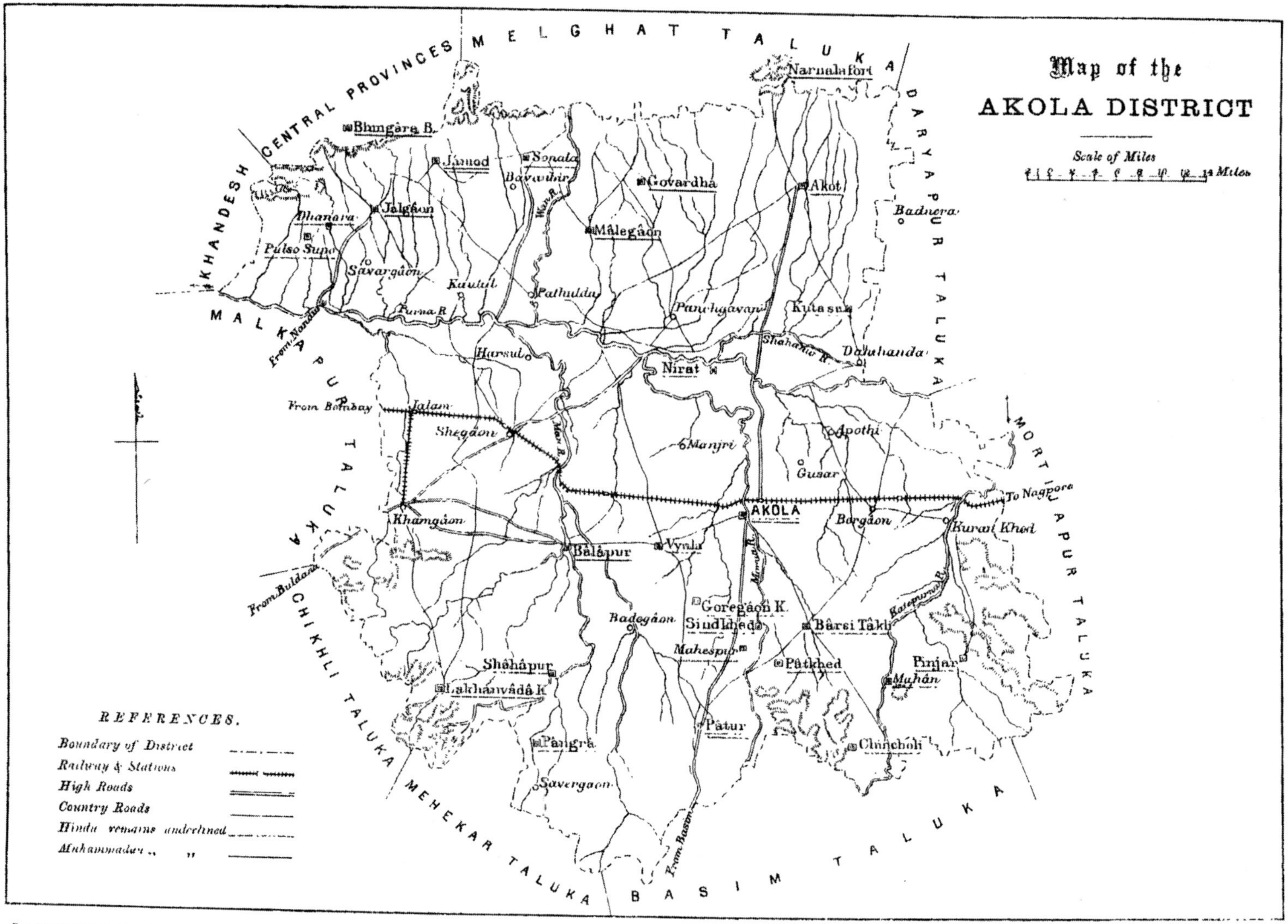

Reg No 610, R & A—Mar 96—410

Litho, S. I. ...

III.—AKOLÂ.

III. 1. **Akolá.** The temple of Śrî Râjeśvara Mahâdeva, about 12 feet square, said to have been built about 300 years ago; built of stone, brick and mortar. A mosque to the south of Akolâ, 30 feet square, of stone and mortar, built about 200 years ago.

III. 2. **Akot,** 28 miles north of Akolâ. The Jami Masjid, 50 feet by 63 feet, said to have been built in the time of the Emperor Alamgir, has 4 lines of inscription. It is in a wretched condition. "Mir Najar's dome" with 4 lines of inscription in Persian, built about 213 years ago, has an *inâm* attached to it. Gada Nârâyaṇa's dome, with 3 lines of inscription in Persian, half a mile to the south of the town in Survey No. 473 on the Kamlâpur road, 30 feet by 30 feet, with a well-built dome.

II*a*. 3. **Bálápur,** 16 miles to west of Akolâ, and 6 miles from Paras railway station. The fort of Bâlâpûr is the largest, and probably the strongest, in Berar, the hill forts of Melghât excepted. It was completed in 1757 A.D. by Ismael Khân, first Nawâb of Elichpur, as we learn from an inscription on the front gate. The Jami Masjid, in the city, was built according to an inscription on one of its stones, in 1622 A.D. It is a fine building, 24 feet by 51 feet. On the bank of the river, to the south of the town, there is a *chhatri* of black stone, supposed to have been built by Savâi Jai Sinha Râjâ, who came with Alamgir to the Dakhan, and was one of his best generals. This edifice is 25 feet square and 38 feet in height. In Kasaikheḍ, a suburb of Bâlâpur, is Khâs Bibi's Mahâl or palace, 19 feet by 20 feet, built of stone and mortar.

II*b*. 4. **Bársi Tákli,** 12 miles south-east of Akolâ. The temple of Śrî Kâlikâ Devî, measuring 42 feet by 27 feet. This is an old "Hemâdpanti" temple of peculiar plan, the shrine being attached sideways to the hall or *maṇḍapa*. It is covered with lines of mouldings and sculptures, but the roof of the hall and spire of the shrine have disappeared. The lower courses of the basement have
III. suffered a great deal. Within is an inscription. Another temple of Śrî Koleśvara Mahâdeva, 54 feet square, the lower portion of stone and the rest of brick.

III. 5. **Bhingára Buzruk,** 9 miles north of Jalgâon. A *mahâl* or palace, 30 feet by 15 feet, supposed to have been built about 150 years ago. It is used by Government officers when on tour.

III. 6. **Chincholi,** 20 miles south of Akolâ. A step-well, 30 feet square. In the jungles to the east of Chincholi the temple of Śrî Rudra Devî, 15 feet square, said to have been built 150 years ago.

III. 7. **Dhanora,** 5 miles south-west of Jalgâon. Temple of Mahâsiddha, 29 feet by 16 feet, built partly of stone and partly of bricks and mortar.

III. 8. **Goregáon Khurd,** 8 miles from Akolâ. A small temple of Mahâdeva ascribed to Hemâdpant, 10 feet by 10 feet.

III. 9. **Govardhá,** 32 miles north of Akolâ. The *dargâh* of Shâl Dâval. Enjoys *inâm* lands assessed at R58, intended for the up-keep of the building.

III. 10. **Jalgáon,** 38 miles north-west of Akolâ. A small *masjid* in the town having an **inscription** partly in Arabic and partly in Persian. The *masjid* has an *inâm* grant.

III. 11. **Jámod,** 6 miles north-east of Jalgâon. Pîr Pawalad Shâh's *dargâh,* said to have been built in the time of Alâu'd-din Ghori, Emperor of Delhi, also a *masjid,* and a temple of Mahâdeva.

12. **Kasaikhed.** *Vide* Bâlâpur.

III. 13. **Kutása,** 24 miles north of Akolâ. Temple of Mahâdeva built of stones without mortar, in fair condition. An **inscription** of 7 lines in *Devanâgari.*

III. 14. **Lakhanvádá,** 18 miles south of Khâmgâon. A stone arch with 5 lines of **inscription** in Persian.

III. 15. **Mahán,** 24 miles south-east of Akolâ. Temple of Karṇeśvara Mahâdeva, 30 feet by 21 feet, built of brick and mortar.

III. 16. **Mahespur,** 8 miles south of Akolâ. Temple of Śrî Kholeśvara Mahâdeva 48 feet by 18 feet, built of stone without mortar, ascribed to Hemâdpant.

III. 17. **Málegáon,** 38 miles north-west of Akolâ. Khaki Shâh's *dargâh.* For its maintenance it has *inâm* land assessed at R23.

IIa. 18. **Narnálá** fortress, 36 miles north of Akolâ. The ramparts have fallen
in several places. There are a few old buildings still standing—(1) The Mahâkâlî
Ia. gate is a particularly well built and decorated building and deserving of delineation.
IIa. Upon it are 3 lines of **inscription** in Persian. (2) A mosque. (3) Ambar *bangalá*
where district officers usually put up. (4) Silekhânâ (armoury). (5) Bârudkhânâ.
(6) Bârâdari *bangalâ.* (7) Lâkud *mahâl.* (8) Sâkhar *talâv,* 105 feet by 240 feet,
which has a good supply of water. (9) Upasâgara *talâv,* 700 feet by 250 feet, con-
taining good water. (10) A *masjid* containing a Persian **inscription** of 4 lines.
Ia. (11) The Shâhanur gateway, a very fine piece of work, on the east of the fort; and
(12) the Delhi gate.

III. 19. **Nirat,** 14 miles north of Akolâ. The temple of Mahâdeva. The lower portion of the temple ascribed to Hemâdpant; the upper rebuilt of brick and mortar.

III. 20. **Palso Supo,** 8 miles south-west of Jalgâon. Temple of Supoba, 20 feet by 19 feet, built of bricks and mortar.

III. 21. **Pángrá,** 16 miles south of Bâlâpur on the Pimpalkhuta road. The temple of Mahâdeva said to have been built by Hemâdpant.

III. 22. **Pátkhed,** 18 miles south of Akolâ. A very old step-well ascribed to Hemâdpant.

III. 23. **Pátur,** 20 miles south of Akolâ. A cave cut in the rock, with one line of inscription. The shrines of a Musalman saint and of a Hindu *sâdhu* are well known and much frequented. Qâzi's *masjid*, 37 feet by 52 feet, built of stone, brick, and mortar.

III. 24. **Pinjar,** 20 miles south-east of Akolâ. A step-well and an old temple of Śrî Kapâleśvara, 72 feet by 54 feet, both ascribed to Hemâdpant, both in good condition. The Gazetteer says there is a Sanskrit inscription upon the temple, but the "returns" give none.

III. 25. **Sháhápur,** 20 miles south-east of Khâmgâon. The ruins of a *mahâl* or palace built by Prince Murâd, son of Akbar, who commanded the province.

III. 26. **Sindkhed,** 11 miles south of Akolâ. The old temple of Śrî Moreśvara, Mahâdeva, 66 feet by 33 feet, and ascribed to Hemâdpant.

III. 27. **Sonála,** 16 miles south-west of Jalgâon, Temple of Śrî Jagadambâ, 27 feet by 24 feet, built of bricks and mortar.

III. 28. **Vyála,** 8 miles east of Bâlâpur. Another temple of Mahâdeva ascribed to Hemâdpant, measuring 75 feet by 105 feet.

IV.—Buldânâ.

III. 1. **Adgáon,** 28 miles to the south-west of Mehkar. An old temple of Mahâdeva with two shrines, the second holding an image of Devî. Built in *chunam* and in good repair.

2. **Amdápur,** 14 miles west of Chikhli, and 20 miles east of Buldânâ. About half a mile to the south of the village is a small hill bordered on the south and south-east by a deep picturesque ravine, and falling out into the plain by gentle undula-
III. tions to the north and west. On the summit of this hill stands a fine modern temple dedicated to Bhavâni, of whom there is an image bedaubed with red lead in the sanctuary which is curiously lit from above in such a way as to throw the full light upon the image, while the spectator sees it only through a chink in the door, and, the *maṇḍapa* being nearly dark, the effect may be somewhat startling to the ignorant. On the temple is an **inscription** of 8 lines. The characters are illegible.

IIb. Near this temple are seen some fragments of a large colossal statue. These are a pair of feet six and half feet from toe to heel, and a hand to match, so that the statue may have been from fifty to sixty feet high. This enormous figure has not been a monolith, but built up in pieces as is evident from the heel being separate from the fore part of the foot which includes the ankles. Over the foot there is an anklet, but there is no indication of the toe-joints or of the extensor muscles over them, while the ankles are on a level with one another. Near them is another pair of feet somewhat smaller. The villagers say that a fine Hemâdpanti temple formerly stood on the site of another temple dedicated to Mahâdeva; and this seems to be confirmed by the fragments built in with it, and lying about in all directions. It is uncared for.

III. 3. **Anjani Buzruk,** 6 miles east of Mehkar. An old temple standing in field No. 146 not far from the village. It is in a good state of preservation. The front hall has eight stone pillars and three stone beams.

III. 4. **Anjani Khurd,** 8 miles south-west of Mehkar. An old step-well with three flights of steps and a little room on the south side, in the village. Also an unfinished
IIb. *masjid* built up solidly to the crowns of the arches all around. In general design the building is similar to the mosque at Fatehkheldâ.

III. 5. **Antri,** in Mehkar *tâlukâ*. Ruins of a Hemâdpanti temple.

III. 6. **Bhadola,** 5 miles east of Buldânâ. An old temple of Mahâdeva, with a fine image of Mahâdeva; out of repair.

III. 7. **Bhokar,** 6 miles west of Chikhli. An old temple of Mahâdeva. The main building is circular (?), the front hall is square.

Reg No 610 R & A—Mar 96—410

Litho., S. I. O., Calcutta.

III. 8. **Bhumrála,** 22 miles south-west of Mehkar. An old temple of Mahâdeva standing in Survey No. 72 with a *bárava* in front.

III. 9. **Borgáon,** 4 miles east of Chikhli. An old ruined temple of Mahâdeva in a field.

III. 10. **Brahmapuri** or Barhanpur, 8 miles north-west of Mehkar. A ruined Hemâdpanti temple on the banks of the Pengangâ river.

II*b*. 11. **Chandol,** 14 miles west of Chikhli. (1) An old temple of Narasinha. The temple stands in Survey No. 55. The principal building is octagonal in form; the hall in front quadrangular. It is profusely sculptured. It has an *inâm* annual rental of R6 for service performed by one Sadâśiv *bin* Keśav Bhat. Repairs are sometimes carried out by subscription. The top has been rebuilt of brick and mortar.
II*b*. (2) Old temple of Mahâlakshmî, in good repair. It is covered with sculpture. It is
III. in charge of Desmukh Amritrâv Vinâyakrâv. (3) An old temple of Mahâdeva. The main building is octagonal, the front hall rectangular. Most of the front hall or
III. *maṇḍapa* has fallen. It has no custodian. And (4) another old temple of Mahâdeva the top of which has been rebuilt of bricks and mortar. It stands in Survey No. 55. The front hall has fallen, and the building is neglected.

III. 12. **Chikhli,** 14 miles south of Buldânâ. A temple of Mahâdeva to the west of the village. The top has been rebuilt (about 25 years ago), other buildings have been added to it.

III. 13. **Chinchkhed.** Ruins of a Hemâdpanti temple.

III. 14. **Daregáon,** 14 miles west of Mehkar, an old temple of Mahâdeva, standing at a little distance from the village. It is surrounded with thick jungle.

III. 15. **Devalgáon Rájá,** 60 miles south of Buldânâ. Formerly there were two old temples here. The town was once fortified by a wall which is now in ruins. This wall had seven approaches—five large gates and two small ones.

III. 16. **Devalghát,** 14 miles north-west of Chikhli. This is a town of considerable antiquity and contains the ruins of numerous Hemâdpanti temples.

III. 17. **Dhalsavangi,** 16 miles west of Chikhli. An old temple of Devî, called Maddari. This has been partly rebuilt. It stands in Survey No. 48 and consists of three shrines. The principal shrine holds the image of Maddari, while the side ones have those of Kâlikâ and Mahâdeva. It is owned by the Mohita family of Dhad. Three large fairs are held here during the year in honour of the deity. There is a service *inâm* of R12. The temple is situated in a picturesque spot in the midst of hills covered with forest, and stands on the way from Buldânâ to Mhaslâ. Also a square masonry cistern into which three separate springs are led through cow-head gargoyles.

III. 18. **Dhotra,** 17 miles south of Chikhli. Two old ruined temples.

III. 19. **Digrás,** 24 miles west of Mehkar. An old temple of Mahâdeva on the east of the village, partly ruined.

III. 20. **Dombrul.** An old temple of Mahâdeva with a raised platform, standing to the north of the village in Survey No. 7. It is ruined.

III. 21. **Dongarsevali,** 10 miles north of Chikhli. An old temple of Mahâdeva standing on Government waste land; ownerless. The central portion is partly sculptured.

III. 22. **Dudha,** 13 miles north-west of Chikhli. A fine Hemâdpanti temple about a mile from the village. On the temple are little *idgâh minârs* to prevent Muhammadans from damaging it.

III. 23. **Dusalbid,** 20 miles south-west of Mehkar. An old temple of Mahâdeva on the north of the village. The hall or *sabhá maṇḍapa* is in ruins.

I*b*. 24. **Fatehkheldá,** 12 miles north-west of Mehkar. Originally called Shakarkheldâ, but subsequently changed to Fatehkheldâ after a pitched battle fought here in 1724 between Nizâm-ul-mulk and Mubariz Khân. Here there is a very fine little *masjid* in excellent preservation. It has a three-arched façade and four free standing pillars. The latter have octagonal shafts with square caps and bases. Simple little rosettes decorate the spandrils of the arches. Nearly all the decoration is above the cornice. The roof has one central dome which stands upon an ornamental octagonal drum and four little lantern *minárs*, one at each corner. The mosque is surrounded by a garden and walled enclosure. It enjoys an *inâm* of R170 for its up-keep.

III. 25. **Girdá,** 8 miles west of Buldânâ. An old temple of Mahâdeva, standing a little distance away from the village.

III. 26. **Giroli,** 30 miles south-west of Chikhli. Said to have Hemâdpanti remains.

III. 27. **Gomedhar,** 14 miles north of Mehkar. An old temple of Mahâdeva. The temple stands in a valley surrounded by hills upon all sides. A fair is annually held here.

III. 28. **Gumi,** 16 miles west of Buldânâ. An old temple of Mahâdeva, in ruins, on the bank of a *nâlá* to the east of the village.

III. 29. **Gundha,** 8 miles south of Mehkar. An old temple of Mahâdeva, to the north of the village. It is in good repair. It has a small *inâm* rental of R3.

III. 30. **Isvi,** 15 miles north-east of Mehkar. An old temple of Vâlkeśvara belonging to the Mânbhavas, on the banks of a *nâlá*, 200 paces from the village. Also an old and without this octagon are embellished with groups of figures; on one a man is playing on a flute, with women and cows on either side; on the next is a figure with four arms trampling on a prostrate form and holding in two upper hands a *chakra* and *konch*, and in the two latter a scimitar and club; there is a woman on one side, two on the other, and in the angles are Hanumân and a cow. In the third is a figure holding a man round the waist between his thighs and apparently crushing his head with his hands, whilst two figures are represented on either side. The last compartment contains a figure with four arms, the two upper raised; one of the lower grasps a man by the hair and the other holds him by the arm, while the right foot is placed on his back. On the right is a woman with clasped hands and a small standing figure on the left, and in the angles behind, prostrate supplicating, a woman.

Above the frieze the dome becomes circular, and consists of three cornices, the lower plain, the next carved with foliage, and the third with geometrical figures; while above all is a rosette in the centre.

The doorway into the shrine is seven feet three inches by three feet eight inches. Round it the ornamentation is exceedingly elaborate, and in the centre over it a figure of Gaṇeśa. The priests object to one's entering the sanctuary, but on the pedestal (apparently original) is an erect statue of Vishṇu with the two arms upraised, the one holding a *konch* and the other a *chakra*, and the other two pendant, the right holding a club and the left a man by the hair. The image is said to have been brought from Nâgpur at very great cost.

Like those of Amruth (Ambarnâtha ?) and Somanâtha, the whole exterior of this temple is one mass of sculpture, and the eaves and some of the borders are very beautiful; but though the quantity of sculpture is so great, the subjects are comparatively few,—gods of the Hindu pantheon, obscenity in its grossest forms, dancing girls and musicians, and all the paraphernalia of debauchery. Many of the groups, visible forty years ago have since been knocked off, a piece of Vandalism similar to that enacted at Elura where several statues were emasculated to save the blushes forsooth of two prudish ladies: but still traces remain to render it a case of "honi soit qui mal-y pense."

II*b*. (2). The next Hemâdpanti temple is to the north of the village, and midway between it and the temple and tank; it consists of a portico with small wings at each end open in front, but enclosed on the other side and supported by three lines of columns and pilasters opposite each column in the third rank. It measures 102 feet by 20 feet, and there has been an enclosed building in a line with one of the wings. It is supposed to have been a place of almsgiving; the recipients occupy the portico while the victuals were cooked in the enclosure.

II*b*. (3). To the east of the large temple is a fine Hemâdpanti tank. It is enclosed by a stone wall eleven feet high, on three sides of which are passages of nine steps leading down to the first terrace, which is 85 feet square. The walls, both of the enclosure and at the sides of the steps, are ornamented with pretty pilasters and niches, whilst on the fourth side is a charming balcony projecting over the first and second terraces.

There are four terraces decreasing in size in proportion with the descent. There are six steps from the first to the second and the third, and from the third to the fourth.

IIb. (4), (5), (6), (7) and (8). Half way along the road to the salt lake is another very pretty temple, and there are four others in the margin of the lake.

All these temples probably belong to about the 12th century when the Hindus seem to have been perfectly "mad upon their idols" and were only saved from utter degradation resulting therefrom by the inroads of the iconoclastic followers of Islâm.

III. 39. **Madh,** 22 miles north-west of Chikhli. An old temple of Mahâdeva, standing at the source of the Pengangâ. It is in ruins.

III. 40. **Malangi,** 6 miles south of Chikhli. An old temple of Mahâdeva.

III. 41. **Malkápur,** a station on the G. I. P. Railway. A temple of Śrî Râmachandra in which there is an illegible inscription of about ten lines in *nâgarî* characters, also the old Jami Masjid.

III. 42. **Masrul,** 20 miles west of Chikhli. An old temple of Mahâdeva, standing in Survey No. I, being used as a *sarâi.*

43. **Mehkar,** 36 miles south-east of Buldânâ. All that a few years ago represented the once fine temple of Mehkar was a picturesque ruin of standing columns and lintels, situated upon a very high basement or platform. The columns, judging from photographs, were of an old type and rather neat in design, and decorated with large lozenge-shaped ornament, conventional eaves, and bands of geese. These have now all disappeared.

In 1888 there was excavated at Mehkar an image of "Bâlâji" (Vishṇu ?). It is a well-carved, highly polished, blackstone image, about life size. He stands with two hands hanging down and two bent upwards. In the right upper he holds the handle of a club with the head of it resting below. The right lower holds a lotus bud; the left upper, the *chakra;* and in the left lower hand he holds the *śankha.* He wears several necklaces, and around his loins hang ornamental chains and hangings. He wears armlets, bracelets, and anklets, and stands upon a lotus. Upon his head is a very high conical bejewelled cap, with the *kírttimukha* set in front and above it a two-armed seated figure with a bow. At his feet on either side are smaller figures—on the right a dwarf with a seated female worshipper with hands together, and on the left a similar dwarf to the last with a taller standing figure. One dwarf holds a *śankha*, whilst the other holds the *chakra*. The standing female figure holds the *padma* or lotus bud. Around the figure is a frame, pointed at the top, upon each side of which are small panels containing the *avatáras* of Vishṇu, four on each side. Above the *avatáras*, on either side, is a little nich, the right holding Brahmâ, the left Śivâ. Behind the head is an ornamental halo. Though elaborately and minutely finished, the style of the figure and features, and a general

stiffness, savour strongly of very late if not quite modern workmanship. The figure most certainly does not belong to the age of the old temple at Mehkar. It is said to have been excavated at Mehkar and to have been found in a buried
III. room. A new temple to enshrine this image has been erected upon the site of the ruins mentioned above.

III. 44. **Mhasle,** 20 miles west of Malkâpur. Said to have a Hemâdpanti temple.

III. 45. **Nagangáon,** 18 miles south of Malkâpur (? 20 miles west of Mehkar). A small temple of Mahâdeva but of little account.

III. 46. **Nágzari,** 7 miles north-west of Mehkar. An old temple of Mahâdeva, among the hills, standing in Survey No. 9. In front of the temple a spring of water flows out through a *gaumukha*.

III. 47. **Nándre,** 10 miles north-west of Chikhli. Said to contain a Hemâdpanti temple.

III. 48. **Náravel,** 7 miles north of Malkâpur. Temple of Koteśvara Mahâdeva. Stands on the banks of the Pûrṇâ, and has *inâm* land for its up-keep.

III. 49. **Panchdevala,** 18 miles north-east of Mehkar; a deserted village. A triple-shrined old temple of Mahâdeva, partly ruined.

III. 50. **Párdá,** 18 miles west of Mehkar (? 6 miles south-west). An old temple of Mahâdeva situated at the foot of a hill. It has *inâm* land rented at R5 for the up-keep of the service in the temple. It is in a ruinous state.

III. 51. **Pimpalgáon Rájá,** 20 miles south-east of Malkâpur. Within the environs of the town, to the southern side, there is a subterranean temple of the goddess Reṇitkâ; it is about 30 feet deep, without masonry, three arches leading into a narrow passage hewn out of the rock; at the bottom is the idol. Close by are three fine cisterns. This temple is said to be prior to the foundation of the town; the goddess used to enjoy some annual allowance, which Aurangzib granted on being convinced by some miracles of the presence of divinity.

III. 52. **Rájegáon,** 10 miles west of Mehkar. An old temple of Mahâdeva of elegant construction. Has a fine image in the shrine. The temple is in good order.

III. 53. **Rájur,** 21 miles south of Malkâpur. An old temple of Râmeśvara in a dilapidated condition.

II*b*. 54. **Rohinkhedá,** 20 miles south of Malkâpur. A temple of Kâleśvara Mahâdeva, partly rebuilt, but much ruined. Also the old Jami Masjid, originally a well-built and decorated building, but now much dilapidated. It has an inscription in Persian characters. The *masjid* is built much on the same plan and lines as that at Fatehkheldâ.

III. 55. **Sákegáon,** 4 miles west of Chikhli. The temple here consists of a closed *maṇḍapa*, shrine, and porch. A large portion of the back of the shrine has fallen with most part of the *śikhara*. The walls are comparatively plain, being decorated by four or five lines of bold moulding round the plinth, surmounted by three bands of ornament. In plan, all angles are right angles and the projecting faces of the *maṇḍapa* walls are shallow. Those of the shrine are bolder but plain and simple in outline. The part of the *śikhara* that stands shews it to have been in the northern style of the same type as that of Govindeśvara at Sinnar.

II*b*. 56. **Sátgáon,** 4 miles north of Chikhli. Five Hemâdpanti temples—(1) The principal one is just outside the west wall of the village, and almost adjoining it. (2) On the north side are the remains of a small but beautiful temple which appears to have been originally in the same enclosure. (3) The other three are close within the village walls; the largest of them is merely an oblong apartment containing the *linga* and *yoni* and an image of Gaṇeśa. There has been a verandah in front supported by four columns; and the entrance has been elaborately sculptured. In the centre of this verandah is a large sculpture of Nandi. (4) The next in size consists of four columns supporting the architraves, above which is the common simple roof. But the backs of the posterior pair of columns being only rough hewn, this may have only been the portico of another temple. (5) The fifth is only a small cell distinguishable as Hemâdpanti only by the pilasters on each side of the entrance.

The principal temple faces the west. The hall is about sixteen feet six inches square with porticoes to the north, south, and west. To the east are the antechamber and sanctuary. In the centre of the hall is the däis, so common in these temples, nine feet (? inches) high and eight feet two inches square, upon the corners of which stand columns two feet square and seven feet ten inches high. Opposite these, at four feet two inches distance on the east side, are pilasters forming the entrance to the vestibule of the shrine, while at the same distance on the other sides are somewhat smaller columns only one foot six inches square at the base and seven feet three inches high. There are another pair forming the fronts of the porticoes which are about five feet wide. All round, the temples and its porticoes are open, with a low screen wall about two feet high, ornamented by dwarf pilasters, between each pair of which are dancing figures. The coping of this screen is a broad slab supported within by brackets ornamented with tigers and elephants' heads outside.

The vestibule of the shrine is six feet wide and four feet four inches deep, on either side of which is a handsome niche in which are the remains of statues. Over the pilasters, on each side the entrance to it, is an extra capital crowned by one elephant, and this is repeated all round the temple. The entrance to the sanctuary is charmingly sculptured, and the whole face is of polished black marble. Gaṇeśa as usual flourishes on the centre of the lintel of the door. The shrine is six feet square, and inside are the remains of a very handsome *vedi* or pedestal also of black marble, but the image it once supported is destroyed and the feet (of alabaster) with anklets around them alone remain.

The four centre columns within the hall are very handsome. The capitals have four brackets each supported by a four-armed figure. The capital rests on an abacus supported by figures at the corners now destroyed. The architraves are all very massive and divided into compartments containing gods and goddesses with attendants. Above this the frieze depicts scenes of combat, wrestling, dancing and musicians, while above is a cornice of pretty foliage, and over that another of scollop pattern. The frieze and cornices form a segment of a circle above which the ceiling is flat and ornamented with a charming pendentive. The architraves over all the outer columns around the temple partake of the same massiveness and richness of carving as the inner ones, and the ceilings between the two are ornamented with the like pendentives. All over the outside of the temples it seems it was profusely sculptured, the principal groups apparently having been in the upper portion, which is now nearly all fallen down.

III. 57. **Sáyakhed,** 30 miles south-west of Mehkar. Said to contain a Hemâdpanti temple.

III. 58. **Sendurjan,** 12 miles west of Mehkar. Three old temples among the hills, one of them with three shrines. Also an old step-well.

III. 59. **Shelgáon,** 14 miles south of Chikhli. An old temple of Mahâdeva.

III. 60. **Shivni,** 32 miles to the south-west of Mehkar. An old temple of Devî, standing upon a hill.

III. 61. **Sinkhed,** 32 miles west of Mehkar. To the north-west of the town the half finished fort stopped by Murshid Khân (about A.D. 1650) still remains an uncompleted structure. It is about 150 yards square, and is built of solid black stone cemented with lead. There are three or four very large wells and tanks, constructed by the Jâdhavs about two hundred years ago, the temple of the god Nîlakaṇṭheśvara, to the south-west, is the oldest structure, supposed to have been built by Hemâdpant, and containing an **inscription** nearly effaced, being some feet under water in the tank near the temple. There are also several palaces, such as the Mahâlbâgh, Mahâkâla, and the Deśmukh's palace, which yet bear testimony to the ancient magnificence of the Jàdhavs, and prosperity of the town. Also the Râmeśvara temple to the west of the town. In an old dome about 50 paces north of the last is a decorated *dargâh* with an **inscription** in five and a half lines on a stone above the doorway.

III. 62. **Sivnagari.** Ruins of a Hemâdpanti temple.

III. 63. **Somathána,** 3 miles east of Chikhli. An old temple of Mahâdeva.

III. · 64. **Sultánpur**, 6 miles south-west of Mehkar. A fine old temple of Mahâdeva partly ruined. An annual fair is held here in the month of Śrâvaṇa, in honour of the deity.

III. ·65. **Tárápur**, 19 miles north of Chikhli, and 8 miles north-east of Buldânâ. An old temple of Devî which stands in Survey No. 6. It is much decayed and has partly fallen. There are inscriptions, each in three lines, in five different places on this temple, but are illegible.

III. ·66. **Umrád**, 26 miles north-west of Mehkar. An old temple of Narasinha.

III. ·67. **Vadáli**, 16 miles north of Mehkar. An old temple of Mahâdeva.

III. ·68. **Vaddári**, 8 miles west of Mehkar. An old temple of Mahâdeva.

III. ·69. **Vadgáon**, 10 miles west of Mehkar. A large old step-well, with two flights of steps one on each side. Upon one side the steps have fallen.

III. 70. **Vághali**. Said to have Hemâdpanti remains.

III. · 71. **Varud**, 20 miles west of Chikhli. An old temple of Mahâdeva in a dilapidated condition.

III. · 72. **Varvand**, 16 miles north of Mehkar. An old temple of Mahâdeva situated among the hills, with a spring near.

III. · 73. **Yeklára**, 8 miles east of Chikhli. An old temple of Mahâdeva.

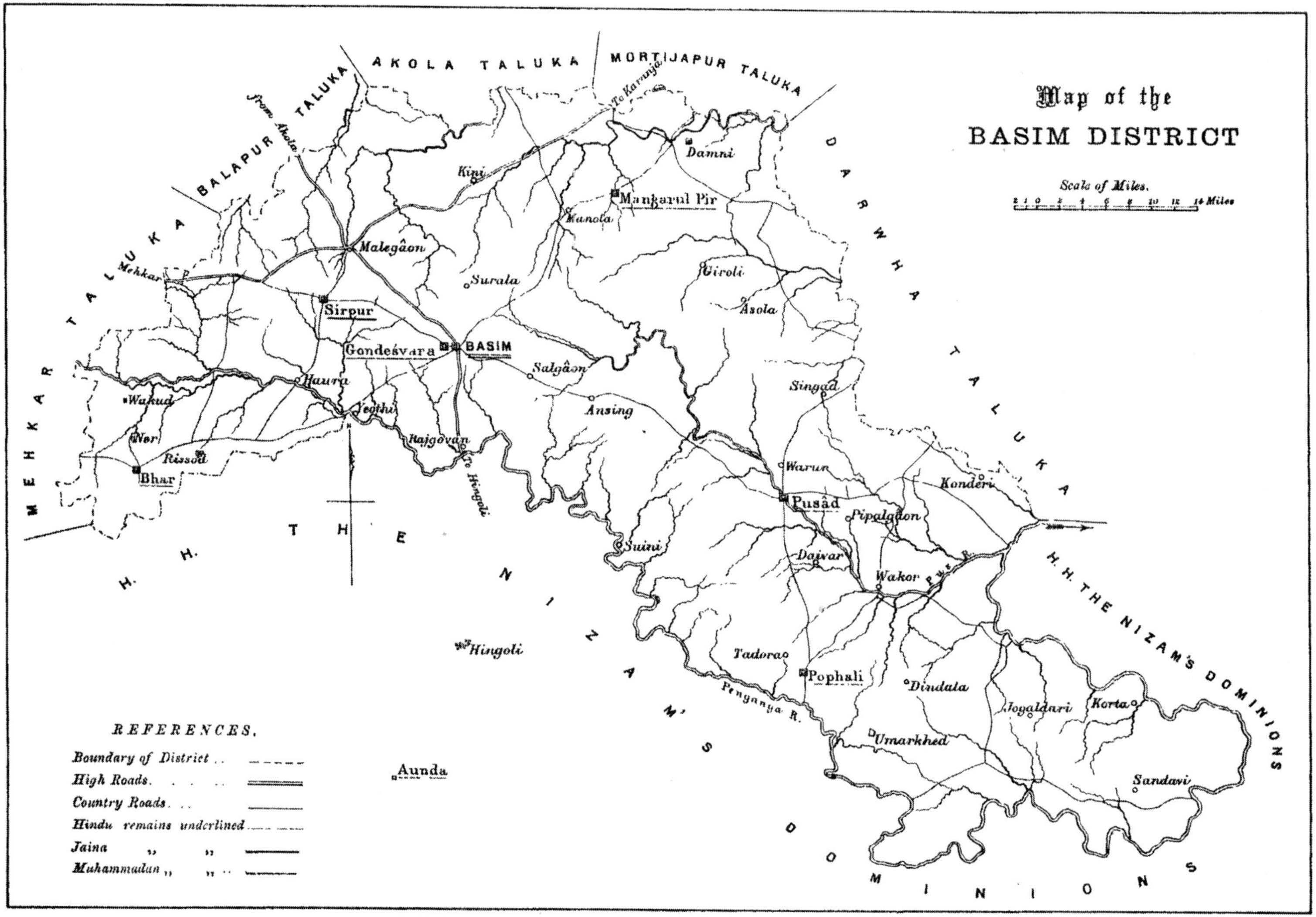

Reg No 610, R. & A.—Mar 96—410

Litho., S. I. O., Calcutta.

V.—BÂSIM.

III. 1. **Básim.** (1) The Hindu temple adjoining the town of Bâsim, dedicated to Venkaṭeśvara, or more familiarly known as Bâlâsâheb, is said to have been constructed by Bhuvani Kalu at an estimated cost of a *lâkh* of rupees. It is a well-built temple and is one of the finest modern temples in Berâr. (2) A small temple of Bâlâji situated in the middle of the town, said to have been constructed 500 years ago, is built of burnt brick and lime and plastered. (3) A small temple of Karṇeśvara Mahâdeva, said to have been built some 200 years ago. (4) *Masjid* of Kaki Shâh in the heart of the town, a plain building of brick and lime.

III. 2. **Aunda-Nágganáth,** 40 miles south of Bâsim in Haidarâbâd territory. A very fine temple covered with statues and sculpture.

III. 3. **Bhar,** 3 miles west by south from Rissod. An old Hindu temple with the tomb of Ratanâtha, supposed to have been built 275 years ago. The temple has *inâm* land attached.

III. 4. **Gomi.** One or two small temples.

III. 5. **Gondeśvara,** a hamlet adjacent to Bâsim. A small temple of Bâlâji in brick and mortar.

III. 6. **Mangarul Pir,** 20 miles north-east of Bâsim. The evidences of old mosques and other buildings partially and wholly in ruins indicate that Mangarul was once a much more prosperous place than it is at present. Upon high ground overlooking the town stands the *dargâh* of Hyat Kalandar. It is said to have been constructed 660 years ago. It is an elegant building but plain. On the left side of the *masjid* is an inscription of 1146. The place enjoys an *inâm* grant of R600 for its up-keep. There are other two *dargâhs* of Shanam Sâheb and Shanamula Sâheb, to the south of the town.

III. 7. **Pophali,** 6 miles north-west of Umarkhed. Near the village are the ruins of a Hemâdpanti *chhatri*. There is also a Hemâdpanti temple half buried in the ground.

III. 8. **Pusád,** 32 miles south-east of Bâsim. The temple of Mahâdeva, a small Hemâdpanti shrine. On the banks of the river Pus, on the road to Bâsim, are the remains of some small Hemâdpanti shrines, and a larger temple of this class has been partly excavated.

III. 9. **Sirpur,** 12 miles west by north of Bâsim. Famous for the shrine of Antariksha Pârśvanâtha, a sacred resort of the Jains. There is here a small but ancient Jaina temple having a horizontal dome with pendants richly carved.

VI.—Wun.

III. 1. **Ashtona,** in Kelâpur *tâluká*. A temple of Mahâdeva.

III. 2. **Bham,** 16 miles south of Yeotmâl on the Aran river. Ruins of immense buildings of stone covering a very large area, and now overgrown with jungle.

III. 3. **Dabhadi,** 25 miles south of Darva. The temple of Omkâreśvara stands a quarter of a mile to the west of the village, ascribed to Hemâdpant. It is 67½ feet long, and the roof is supported upon 28 plain octagonal columns. It is in a ruined condition. In front is a *dîpamâla* and a *samâdhi* or tomb sculptured with monkeys.

III. 4. **Darva** contains some old tombs belonging to the Qâzi's family which are beautifully built in a fine-grained stone.

III. 5. **Dudhgáon,** 2 miles east of Darva. The temple of Śrî Panchalingeśvara consists of a shrine and *sabhâ maṇḍapa,* and is supported in part by eighteen columns of black stone. The *sabhâ maṇḍapa* is enclosed upon three sides but open on the fourth, and around the walls are niches. The temple is ascribed to Hemâdpant.

III. 6. **Javalgáon,** 9 miles north-east of Darva. An old ruined Hemâdpanti temple of Mahâdeva. The roof of the *sabhâ maṇḍapa* is supported upon twelve columns four of which are enclosed. In the centre of the *sabhâ maṇḍapa* is a tortoise carved in stone.

III. 7. **Jugad,** 14 miles south of Wun. A Hemâdpanti temple whose roof is supported by twenty-two columns, most of them sculptured. The temple appears to have once been a very good one, but it is going to ruin.

III. 8. **Kalam,** in Yeotmâl *tâluká,* has an underground temple dedicated to Chintâmaṇ.

III. 9. **Kalamner** in Kelâpur *tâluká*. An old Hemâdpanti temple of Mahâdeva.

III. 10. **Kap,** on the Pengangâ, 30 miles west of Pândarkauda. A temple to Kâpeśvara, but not old.

III. 11. **Kelápur,** 28 miles west of Wun. Said to contain a Hemâdpanti temple of Devî.

III. 12. **Kurhád,** 25 miles north-west of Kelâpur. A Hemâdpanti temple of Mahâdeva.

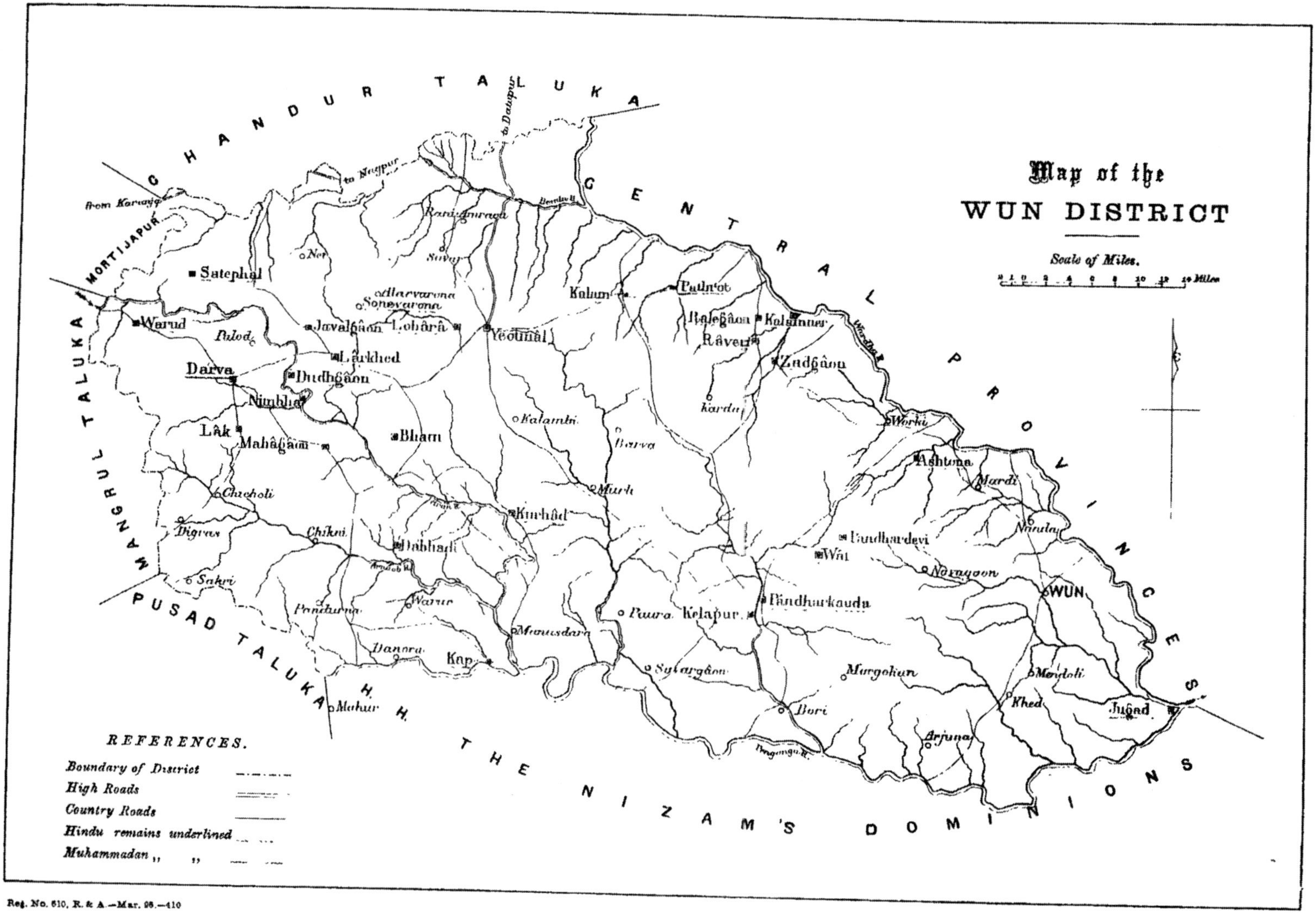

Reg. No. 610, R. & A.—Mar. 98.—410

Litho., S. I. O., Calcutta.

III. 13. **Lák,** 6 miles south of Darva. A double Hemâdpanti temple. Two shrines face one another and are joined by a common *sabhá maṇḍapa*. The eastern portion of the temple is in ruins, but the western is in a comparatively good condition.

III. 14. **Lárkhed,** about 10 miles east of Darva. An old Hemâdpanti temple of Laksheśvara Mahâdeva consists of a shrine and *sabhá maṇḍapa* supported upon sixteen carved pillars.

III. 15. **Lohárá,** 2½ miles from Yeotmâl. An old temple ascribed to Hemâdpant consisting of sanctum and *sabhâ maṇḍapa,* the latter being supported upon eighteen black stone columns, six of which are sculptured.

III. 16. **Mahágáon,** 11 miles south-east of Darva. An old temple of Kamaleśvara Mahâdeva consisting of a shrine and *sabhá maṇḍapa* supported by eighteen columns, twelve of which are enclosed. Both sides of the entrance to the temple are well carved.

III. 17. **Nimbha,** 9 miles east of Darva. An old temple with a subterranean hall, the roof of which is supported by sixteen columns, twelve of which are enclosed. The walls, on either side of the entrance to the underground chamber, are sculptured. In the underground room are placed the image of "Śrî Dattâtreya" and the ten incarnations of Vishṇu. The temple is held in great sanctity by the Hindus, who here offer their oblations to the manes of their deceased ancestors.

III. 18. **Pándarkauda** in Wun *tâluká*. A temple to Muradhar (? Muralidhara) but apparently modern.

III. 19. **Pándhardevi** in Kelâpur *tâluká,* situated in reserved State forest. Said to be a Hemâdpanti temple.

III. 20. **Páthrot,** 50 miles east of Darva. The temple of Śrî Devî Lakhamjâi, situated to the west of the village, ascribed to Hemâdpant but said to have been repaired by one of the Râjâs of Nâgpur. Sixteen columns support the *sabhá maṇḍapa,* but they are plain.

III. 21. **Rálegáon** in Kelâpur *tâluká*. Temple of Śrî Rukhumâbâi, modern, and of no special interest.

III. 22. **Ráveri,** 28 miles north of Pândarkauda. An old temple of Mahâdeva, the roof of which is supported by about sixteen columns. The temple is going to ruin.

III. 23. **Sátephal,** 13 miles north of Darva. The temple of Kapileśvara consisting of a shrine and *sabhá maṇḍapa*. The roof is supported by eighteen columns, sixteen of which are enclosed. There are some **inscriptions** on the wall. The walls are sculptured and the doorway is decorated with figures of Kṛishṇa, the eighth incarnation of Vishṇu, surrounded by *gopis*.

III. 24. **Sonevarona,** 16 miles north of Darva. A Hemâdpanti temple, the roof of which is supported by twelve columns, six of which are enclosed, the remaining six being octagonal.

III. 25. **Wái** in Kelâpur *táluká*. A Hemâdpanti temple.

III. 26. **Warud,** 10 miles north-west of Darva. A Hemâdpanti temple to Mahâdeva, the roof of which is supported by six octagonal columns and ten pilasters. In the *sabhá maṇḍapa* are six niches. Repaired some 75 years ago.

III. 27. **Yeotmál.** An old Hemâdpanti temple the roof of which is supported by eighteen pillars, two of which have elephants carved upon them, and the remaining sixteen have carved capitals and bases. The doorway is also sculptured, and upon each side of the entrance are carved niches.

III. 28. **Zadgáon** in Kelâpur *táluká*. An old Hemâdpanti temple of Mahâdeva.

GLOSSARY.

A

Achaleśvara. An epithet of Śiva (the immoveable).
Âditya. The Sun.
Agastya. The name of a celebrated Ṛishi.
Âmalaka. A kind of fruit, and hence used as the name of the crowing member, next the finial, of a *śikhara* or spire on account of its resemblance to that fruit.
Amaranâtha. A name of Śiva.
Ambâi. The name of a goddess.
Ambikâ. A name of Pârvati or Umâ.
Ananta—Sajja. Probably the corruption of Ananta—Śayya, one who rests upon Ananta the snake; hence, Vishṇu.
Antarâla. Antechamber.
Antariksha. The sky.
Ârti. The presentation of a light at the end of the ceremony of worship of an image.
Âśâ. Hope, desire.
Âśâpûraṇi. A goddess who fulfils desires.
Âshâdha. Name of the fourth month of the Hindu year.
Aśvathâman. Name of a famous Brâhmaṇ warrior and General of the army of the Kauravas. He was the son of Droṇâchârya.
Avatâra. An incarnation.
Ayodhyâ. Name of a city, the capital of Râma.

B

Badarinâtha. Name of a temple at Badari dedicated to Vishṇu.
Bâdal Mahâl. Cloud palace.
Bâgeśvara. Śiva.
Bahiṇa—Bhâu. Sister and brother.
Bâlâji. A form of Vishṇu.
Bâlukeśvara. An epithet of Śiva.
Bangalâ. House or Residence.
Bârâdari. A building with 12 doors; a palace.
Bârâlingas. The twelve famous (Jyotir) *lingas* of Śiva.
Bârava. A step-well.
Barudkhânâ. A magazine.
Bâvali. A step-well.
Bhadrâchallam. Name of a mountain.
Bhadrâvati. Name of an ancient city.
Bhadrinâtha. Epithet of Śiva.
Bhairava. Śiva in his terrific form.
Bhavâni. A name of Pârvatî.
Bhûtanâtha. An epithet of Śiva (lord of spirits).
Bîjak. An inscribed slab.
Bindu. A drop.
Birinchi Nârâyaṇa. The sun god.
Brahmâ. The Creator; the first god of the Triad.
Brahmachâri. One who has taken the vow of celibacy.
Brahmapura. Name of a temple.
Buddha. The title of Śâkya Muni, the founder of the Buddhist religion.

C

Chabutrâ. A platform.
Chaitra. The first month of the Hindu year.
Chakra. The discus of Vishṇu.
Champâ. The name of a temple.
Chânde. Name of a celebrated Rajput bard.
Charaṇa. The foot, footprints.
Chaitanyeśvara. An epithet of Śiva.
Chedi. Name of an ancient dynasty in Northern India.
Chintâmaṇi. The philosopher's stone. Also the name of a god
Chowk. A quadrilateral place. A platform.
Chhattri. An umbrella. A small pavilion on pillars.
Chhotâ. Small.

D

Dakhan. The Southern Country.
Dâneśvara. An epithet of Śiva.
Ḍanteśvari. The name of a *devî* (Kâli).
Dargâh. A Musalman tomb.
Darwâza. A gateway.
Daśaratha. Râma's father, King of Ayodhyâ.
Daśa Avatâra. Ten incarnations. Usually applied to the principal ten incarnations of Vishṇu.

Dattâtreya. The name of a sage, son of Atri by his wife Anasûyâ, considered as the incarnation of Brahmâ, Vishṇu, and Śiva.

Davul Durlâ. Name of a temple, named after a queen.

Deval. A temple.

Devanâgari. The style of characters in which Sanskrit is usually written.

Devi. Goddess.

Devikâ-sthâna. Place of a *devî.*

Dhableśvara. Epithet of Śiva.

Dharmapa. Religious austerity.

Dharmaśâlâ. Charity-hall. A shelter built for the free use of travellers and pilgrims.

Dharameśvara. An epithet of Śiva.

Dîpadâna. A lamp-post or pillar, usually a masonry erection with niches for a great number of lights, set up before a temple.

Divân. Prime minister.

Durgâ. A name of one of the forms of Pârvatî.

Dvâra. A doorway.

E

Ekniri. The goddess of Malapur, C.P. (Reṇukâ).

F

Fasli. The Persian era.

G

Gadâ. A mace.

Gaṇapati or Gaṇeśa. The elder son of Mahâdeva, represented with an elephant's head, and god of wisdom.

Gandheśvara. An epithet of Śiva.

Garha. A fort or citadel.

Garuda. A bird, sometimes represented as a man with a bird's head, and a man with a bird's beak; the vehicle of Vishṇu.

Gomukha. A gargoyle in the shape of a cow's head, usually placed at the sources of sacred streams for the water to run through.

Gavali. A milkman.

Ghât. A flight of steps, usually by a tank or river side. A pass in a chain of mountains.

Godâvarî. Name of a river.

Gond. An aboriginal tribe.

Gopâla Deva. Kṛishṇa.

Gopinâtha. Kṛishṇa.

Gudi. A temple.

Gupta. Name of an ancient dynasty.

H

Hanumân. The mythological monkey warrior who assisted Râma.

Hari. A name of Vishṇu.

Hari-Śamkara. Vishṇu-Śiva.

Havêli. A palace.

Hemâdpant. Name of the *divân* of one of the Yâdava kings who is supposed to have built 300 temples as penance for sin.

Hidimba. A demon whose sister became the wife of Bhîma.

Hiraṇya Kaśipu. A demon king slain by Narasinha.

I

Idgâh. A Muhammadan place of prayers.

Ikshu. Sugarcane.

Inâm. Landed property generally given for service rendered.

Indra. The Lord of gods.

J

Jagannâtha. Epithet of Vishṇu as 'Lord of the Universe.'

Jain. A follower of the Jaina religion.

Jami. Assembly, as applied to the chief mosque of a town; sometimes the chief mosque is called the Juma—(Friday) mosque.

Jamindâr. A landlord.

Jatrâ. A fair.

Jharukâ. An air-hole, a window.

Jogi or Yogin. A Hindu religious mendicant; an ascetic.

K

Kabar. A Muhammadan tomb.
Kâla-Bhairava. Śiva in one of his terrible forms.
Kalavantin. A dancing woman.
Kâleśvara. An epithet of Mahâdeva.
Kâli or Kâlikâ. An epithet of Pârvatî as Durgâ.
Kamaleśvara. An epithet of Śiva.
Kamâvisdâr. A subordinate revenue officer.
Kapâleśvara. An epithet of Śiva.
Kâpeśvara. An epithet of Śiva.
Kapila. Name of an ancient sage.
Kapileśvara. An epithet of Śiva.
Karmeśvara. An epithet of Śiva.
Karṇeśvara. An epithet of Śiva.
Kârtika. The seventh month of the Hindu year.
Katorâh. A beggar's bowl.
Keśavanâtha. The god Vishṇu.
Khalâri Mâtâ. Name of a village deity at Khoprâ.
Kholeśvara. An epithet of Śiva.
Khoprâ. Name of a deity at the village of the same name.
Kîrttimukha. 'Face of Fame.' A grinning face much used upon Hindu temples, and is found generally upon the front of the threshold of temple doorways.
Koleśvara. An epithet of Śiva.
Koteśvara. An epithet of Śiva.
Kothi. A store-house, a granary, a room.
Kuleśvara. An epithet of Śiva.
Kuṇḍa. A tank.
Kuśaleśvara. An epithet of Śiva.

L

Lâkh. 1,00,000.
Lakhamjâi. Name of a Goddess.
Lakshaṇeśvara. An epithet of Śiva.
Laksheśvara. An epithet of Śiva.
Lakshmaṇa. Step-brother of Râma, King of Ayodhyâ.
Lakshmi-Nârâyaṇa. Lakshmi and her husband Vishṇu.
Lâkuda-Mahâl. A wooden palace.
Lankeśvari. Name of a goddess.
Lât. A round stone pillar.
Linga. The phallic emblem of Śiva.
Lokapâla (Lokabâla). An epithet of Vishṇu.

M

Maddari. Name of a goddess.
Madhu. Honey.
Madhu Sudhâ. 'Honey and nectar,' name of a *tîrtha*.
Mahâbhârata. The celebrated epic which describes the contests between the sons of Pâṇḍu and Dhṛitarâshtra.
Mahâbodhi. An epithet of Buddha.
Mahâdeva. Śiva, 'the great god.'
Mahâkâla. Śiva in his character as destroyer.
Mahâkâlî. An epithet of Durgâ, the female counterpart of Mahâkâla.
Mahâkosala. Ancient name of a country.
Mahâl. A palace.
Mahâlakshmî. The goddess of fortune.
Mahâmaṇḍapa. The great or main hall of a temple.
Mahâr. A low caste person.
Mahârâja. King; *lit.* 'great king.'
Mahâśivarâtri. The festival in honour of Śiva on the 14th of the dark half of the month of Mâgha.
Maheśvara. An epithet of Śiva.
Mahishâsura-Mardanî. A *devî* who killed the demon Mahishâsura.
Mânbhavas. A religious sect, worshippers of Kṛishṇa, who wear black garments.
Maṇḍapa. A hall in a temple.
Mandira. A temple, mansion, hall.
Mâṇikas. Beads.
Mansarobar (mânasa sarovara). Name of a tank.
Mârkaṇḍa. Name of an ancient sage.
Mâruti. The famous monkey warrior.
Masjid. A mosque.
Maṭha. A monastery.
Moreśvara. An epithet of Śiva.
Mṛikaṇḍu. Name of an ancient sage.
Mṛityunjaya. An epithet of Śiva.
Mukundarâja. Name of a sage and poet.
Mundali. A wall.
Muralidhara. An epithet of Kṛishṇa.
Mushaka (moksha). Final beatitude.

N

Naga. A serpent.
Nagarakhânâ. The place where drums and music are played.
Nâlâ. A small stream.
Nandi. The sacred bull, Śiva's vehicle.
Nandikeśvara. Same as Nandi.

Nanesvara. An epithet of Śiva.
Narasinha. The fourth (lion) incarnation of Vishṇu.
Narasinhanâtha. Same as Narasinha.
Nârâyaṇa. An epithet of Vishṇu.
Nemnûk. Allowance or pension.
Nîlakaṇṭha, Nîlakaṇṭheśvara. Epithets of Siva.
Nimbâi. Name of a goddess.

O

Oṁkâra. The sacred syllable.
Oṁkâreśvara. Epithet of Śiva.

P

Padma. A lotus.
Padmâsanî. A name of Lakshmî.
Padmeśvarî. A name of Lakshmî.
Pahâr or Pahâd. A hill.
Panchalinga. A collection of five *lingas.*
Panchalingeśvara. An epithet of Śiva.
Panchâyatanam. A collection of five shrines, devoted generally to Śiva, Vishṇu, Gaṇeśa, Devî, and Sûrya respectively.
Pâṇḍavas. The five sons of Pâṇḍu.
Paṇḍharinâtha. The famous god Viṭhobâ of Pandharpur.
Pâpavimochana. 'Emancipation from sin;' name of a *tírtha.*
Parganâ. A province.
Pârśvanâtha. One of the 24 Jaina saints.
Patmâheśvarî. An epithet of Pârvatî.
Piṇḍi. A *linga*, the phallic emblem.
Pinglâi. Name of a goddess.
Pippala or pipal. A tree of the fig species.
Pradakshiṇâ. Circumambulation about a shrine.
Pradhâna. A minister of a king.
Pûjâri. A worshipper, more especially one who attends upon the idol to carry out the needful ceremonies.
Puṇḍalîka. One form of Vishṇu, Viṭhobâ.
Purâṇas. Hindu mythological books.
Purâṇika. One who expounds the sacred books.
Pushkariṇi. A lake.

R

Râjâ. King.
Râja-râjeśvara. Kubera.
Râjeśvara. An epithet of Śiva.
Râjîva-lochana. Lotus-eyed.
Râkshasa. A demon.
Râma. The famous King of Ayodhyâ, hero of the Râmâyaṇa, and seventh incarnation of Vishṇu.
Râmachandra. Another name of Râma.
Râmakshetra. Râma's abode.
Râma's tekari. Râma's hill.
Rameśvara. An epithet of Śiva.
Rângoli. Silicious stone powdered.
Râni. Queen.
Ratha. A chariot.
Reṇukâ. Name of the mother of Paraśurâma, 6th incarnation of Vishṇu.
Revâ. A name of the Narmadâ river.
Revâ Nâyaka. 'Lord of the Narmadâ.'
Ṛishi. A sage.
Rudra Devî. A name of Pârvatî.
Rudreśvara. An epithet of Śiva.
Rukhumâi or Rukhumâbâi. Wife of Viṭhobâ.

S

Sabhâ-maṇḍapa. Chief hall of a temple.
Sadâ-badâ. Always great.
Sâdhu. A saint.
Sâkhar. Sugar.
Samâdhi. A tomb.
Sâmba-Śiva. Pârvatî and her husband Śiva.
Śaṁkara. Śiva.
Samlâi. Name of a goddess.
Sâmleśvara. An epithet of Śiva.
Saṁvat. The Vikramâditya Era.
Śankha. The conch shell.
Sati. A woman who immolates herself upon her husband's pyre.
Satya (Yuga). The first of the four Hindu ages.
Savantai. Name of a temple at Savantpur.
Śesha. The great snake deity upon which Vishṇu is often represented as reclining.
Siddheśvara. An epithet of Śiva.
Śikhara. The tower or spire of a temple.
Silekhâna. An armoury.
Sindûragiri. Name of a hill (lit. 'hill of red lead').

Sitâ. Wife of Râma, daughter of Janaka, King of Mithilâ.
Sivarâtri. The Hindu festival in honour of Śiva, held on the 14th day of the dark half of the month of Mâgha.
Somanâtha. An epithet of Śiva.
Someśvara. An epithet of Śiva.
Somleśvara. An epithet of Śiva.
Śrâvaṇa. The fifth month of the Hindu year.
Sthâna. A place, locality.
Stûpa. A Buddhist monument in which relics are deposited, generally of the shape of a mound.
Subhedâr. A district revenue officer.
Śuddha (Paksha). Bright half of the month.
Sudhâ. Nectar.
Śûdra. A man of the 4th or last of the principal Hindu castes.
Sûrya, Sûrja Nâryaṇa, or Sûraj Narayaṇa. The Sun as a deity.
Sûrya Vaṁśi. The Solar race.

T

Tehsil. Subdivision of a district.
Tâkâ. A tank, a rock-cut cistern.
Tâl. A tank.
Talâv. A tank.
Tâṇḍava. A celebrated dance of Śiva.
Tapah. Religious austerity.
Tapasvibâvâkikho. A solitary place of an ascetic.
Tapogiri. A mountain where religious austerities were performed.
Taptajhara. A hot spring.
Tirtha. A holy spot, generally where there is a sacred spring, or tank.
Tretâ (Yuga). The second of the four Hindu ages.
Triśûla. A trident.
Tryaṁbakeśvara. An epithet of Śiva.

U

Umâ-Maheśvara. Pârvatî and Śiva.
Upa sâgara. A small sea, a gulf.

V

Vaidya. A physician.
Vaishṇava. Relating to Vishṇu.
Vajrapâṇi. One having a thunderbolt in his hand, one of the Buddhist Bodhi-sattvas.
Vakratuṇḍa. An epithet of Ganeśa.
Vâlkeśvara. An epithet of Śiva.
Vâmana. The Dwarf *avatâra* of Vishṇu.
Varâha. The Boar *avatâra* of Vishṇu.
Vasisṭha. The name of a sage who was the family priest of Râma.
Venkaṭeśa, Venkaṭeśvara. An epithet of Vishṇu.
Virinchi—Nârâyaṇa. The Sun as a deity.
Vishṇu. The second deity of the Triad, the preserver.
Viṭṭhala. A form of Vishṇu.
Viṭhobâ. A form of Vishṇu.

Y

Yama Darmarâja. The god of death.
Yogin. *Same as* Jogi.
Yoni. The female organ of generation, and represented as combined with the *linga.*
Yuga. An age of the world.

Z

Zamindâr. *Same as* Jamindâr.

INDEX.

A

B

C

H

I

J

K

L

M

N

O

P

R

S

T

U

V

W

Y

Z